Indigenous Peoples

Cover illustration: part of the delegation attending the first international conference on indigenous issues held at the United Nations, Geneva, 1977.

Indigenous Peoples

A Global Quest for Justice

A Report for the Independent Commission on International Humanitarian Issues

Foreword by
Sadruddin Aga Khan and Hassan bin Talal

Zed Books Ltd
London and New Jersey

This report does not necessarily reflect the views, individually or collectively, of the members of the Independent Commission on International Humanitarian Issues (ICIHI). It is based on research carried out for ICIHI and was prepared under the supervision of its Secretariat with the guidance of the ICIHI Working Group on the Indigenous Peoples.

Indigenous Peoples was first published by Zed Books Ltd.,
57 Caledonian Road, London N1 9BU and
171 First Avenue, Atlantic Highlands, New Jersey 07716, in 1987.

Cover design by Henry Iles
Cover photograph credit: Richard Bancroft
Typeset by EMS Photosetters, Rochford, Essex
Printed and bound in Great Britain by Cox and Wyman Ltd., Reading

British Library Cataloguing in Publication Data

Indigenous peoples: a global quest for justice:
a report for the Independent Commission on
International Humanitarian Issues.
1. Native races
I. Independent Commission on International
Humanitarian Issues
305.8   GN380

ISBN 0-86232-758-X
ISBN 0-86232-759-8 Pbk

Contents

The Independent Commission on International Humanitarian Issues

Other ICIHI Reports*

FAMINE: A Man-Made Disaster? (Pan Books, London/ Sydney, 1985; American edition, Random House, New York). Other language editions: Arabic, French, Italian, Japanese, Portuguese, Serbo-Croatian and Spanish.

STREET CHILDREN: A Growing Urban Tragedy (Weidenfeld & Nicolson, London, 1986). Other language editions: Arabic, French, Indonesian, Italian, Japanese, Serbo-Croatian, Spanish and Thai.

THE ENCROACHING DESERT: The Consequences of Human Failure (Zed Books, London/New Jersey, 1986 and College Press, Harare, 1986). Other language editions: Arabic, French and Russian.

THE VANISHING FOREST: The Human Consequences of Deforestation (Zed Books, London/New Jersey, 1986 and College Press, Harare, 1986). Other language editions: French, Russian, Serbo-Croatian and Spanish.

DISAPPEARED: Technique of Terror (Zed Books, London/ New Jersey, 1986). Other language editions: French, Indonesian, Russian and Spanish.

MODERN WARS: The Humanitarian Challenge (Zed Books, London/New Jersey, 1986). Other language editions: French, Japanese and Russian.

REFUGEES: Dynamics of Displacement (Zed Books, London/ New Jersey, 1986). Other language editions: Arabic, French, Indonesian, Russian, Spanish and Thai.

* in addition to the Commission's Final Report.

Other reports to be published include:

ICIHI Working Group on Indigenous Peoples

The following members of the Independent Commission helped in the preparation of this Report in their individual capacities:

Paulo Evaristo Arns	(Brazil)
Henrik Beer	(Sweden)
Manfred Lachs	(Poland)
Willibald P. Pahr	(Austria)
Gough Whitlam	(Australia)
Ru Xin	(China)

Drafting Committee

Z. Rizvi	J. Burger
(Co-ordinator)	(Editor)
R. Dunbar Ortiz	G. Alfredsson
(Consultant)	(Adviser)

Foreword

For most people, the image that the term 'indigenous' evokes is one of 'primitive' people – survivors from an era untouched by 'enlightenment' and 'scientific progress'. The most common image, popularised by Hollywood, is that of the feathered Red Indian fighting the white man.

In the age of mass production and increasing uniformity, we seek pleasure in the 'primitive'. It is not a new phenomenon – so did Rousseau in the 18th century, Gauguin in the 19th, Jung early in this century.

Hidden behind the stereotypes, however, is the stark reality which calls for empathy and challenges our humanity. It is at once grim and bright: on the one side, colonisation, genocide, and a constant struggle for cultural and physical survival; on the other, a glorious past and a future which is slowly but surely beginning to look bright.

Attitudes are changing. Is this any wonder, if we step back for a moment to assess the balance-sheet of material progress? Our technological and social achievements seem precarious in a world which edges ever closer to nuclear armageddon, whose environment is collapsing, where individuals feel increasingly alienated and governments ever less tolerant of diversity and non-conformity.

As we survey the social, environmental and humanitarian fall-out of industrial development, it is occurring to more of us, indigenous and itinerant alike, that we may have some urgent practical lessons to learn, if it is not already too late, from societies which have succeeded in managing a sustainable environment for millenia.

Indigenous peoples have a custodial attitude toward land and life, which respects inter-generational rights. During this century, an ever growing demand, particularly from industrial nations, for natural resources has spurred a global search for untapped reserves. Once thought of as barren wastelands of little economic value, the unexploited territories of indigenous peoples have been identified as areas of rich timber, minerals and river valleys. In the name of development, forests are being removed, mining projects started and dams built, forcing indigenous people out of their traditional habitat.

With a tradition of collective ownership, and, therefore, lacking clear title to the land they inhabit, indigenous peoples are unable to stop these incursions. Thus the alienation from the land which began with colonisation has continued under a different guise for the indigenous. Their common cause is bringing them ever closer to each other in this global village. Their organisations are becoming increasingly active in gaining support and recognition by the world community. By demanding international access, they are challenging those traditional modes of international behaviour which contributed to domination and oppression that for so long have been their lot. Indigenous peoples have been marginalised and exploited. Now, they are resisting as new assaults are carried out against them. They are struggling for survival as peoples, and they need the support of all those who believe in fundamental human rights.

Widespread education about the situation of the indigenous is called for. A starting point would be a thorough review of national histories. Governments should recognise the human tragedy brought about in the past by the unrelenting oppression of these peoples. They should acknowledge the right of the indigenous to be themselves, to have a voice and to pursue their aspirations, whether these be the preservation of their culture and traditions, the management of their lands or, indeed, education and development as they perceive it.

The right of people to be different must be recognised not just as a legal, philosophical or political principle. It is the cornerstone upon which the rich diversity of our planet depends. Without it, we are all the poorer.

It is hoped that this Report, in addition to informing the

general public, will help policy-makers and others whose actions adversely affect the lives of indigenous peoples to redress the situation.

Hassan bin Talal   **Sadruddin Aga Khan**
Co-Chairmen, ICIHI.

Editorial Note

There is no universally accepted description or definition of indigenous peoples. But whether they are called indigenous, autochthonous, tribal, Fourth World or First Nations, there is a growing consensus about them and their continuing plight. Their own perception of themselves combined with the historical fact of being the descendants of the original inhabitants of the lands where they live is enough for anyone to get a fairly precise idea of the subject of this Report. The controversial question of definition is discussed in the Report but we chose to use the term 'Indigenous' because it is the one most commonly known. It is used in the pages that follow in a broad, global sense and includes groups that in some countries may be called tribal or semi-tribal people.

The humanitarian issues relating to indigenous peoples have understandably received the special attention of the Independent Commission and were referred to in practically all its meetings. Detailed discussions of specific aspects took place at two of the Commission's plenary meetings held in the Hague and Tokyo. This Report reflects the deliberations of the Commission and the research done for it by its Secretariat.

In the preliminary phase, the Secretariat commissioned a series of research papers from recognised experts, both indigenous and non-indigenous, on specific aspects of indigenous issues. These facilitated the process of analysis and reflection by the Commission and may be made available separately. We wish to express our appreciation in particular to M. Colchester, S. Corry, A. Eide, R. Plant, R. Stavenhagen and I. Tosevski. The Secretariat's work was facilitated by R-M.

Abi-Saab and R. Dunbar Ortiz. The advice and encouragement of A. Eide who was then Chairman of the UN Working Group on Indigenous Populations was most helpful. During the first meeting of the Independent Commission's Working Group, held in Strasbourg, the participation of several of the above mentioned experts as well as I. Brownlie, M. Davis, R. Falk and K. George greatly benefited the work.

In preparing this Report, extensive use has been made of the relevant United Nations and International Labour Office reports as well as those of indigenous and other non-governmental organisations. The reports of the UN Working Group on Indigenous Populations, chaired by Dr. Erika Irene Daes, were particularly useful. The advice and insights from a number of indigenous representatives helped improve the draft which also benefited from valuable comments by G. Alfredsson, J. Forbes, B. Kingsbury and T. Ranger.

Special tribute is due to J. Burger who, as editor, brought knowledge, experience and enthusiasm to this project of the Commission. The perceptive contributions of R. Dunbar Ortiz during the final stages are also gratefully acknowledged.

The technical work within the Secretariat on all successive drafts was patiently and diligently carried out by D. Mahalic, M. Fitzgerald, M. Jacometti, M-J. Louis and B. Smit.

Finally, we wish to thank Zed Books and, in particular, Robert Molteno, for the speedy publication of this book.

As this Report was being finalised, one of the distinguished members of the Commission, Henrik Beer, who also served on the Working Group on Indigenous Peoples, passed away. We lost in him a man of exemplary commitment to humanitarian causes. From the hospital, during the brief but painful illness which claimed his life, he sent to the Secretariat his written comments on the final draft of this Report. His last sentence read: 'The indigenous need peace and understanding as much as everyone else.' This Report is dedicated to his memory.

Income from the sales of this book will be entirely devoted to research and dissemination of humanitarian issues.

Z. Rizvi
Secretary-General
ICIHI

Geneva, 30 June 1987

Prologue

*'That men do not learn very much from the lessons of history is the
most important of all lessons that history has to teach.'*

Aldous Huxley, 1959

During the United Nations General Assembly session in New
York in 1982, Spain together with some European and *all* the
American states proposed that 1992 be designated by the
United Nations as the year of official commemoration of the
arrival of Cristobal Colon (Christopher Columbus) to America,
marking a 500 year anniversary. Nothing surprising except,
perhaps, the broad political spectrum of supporters of the
proposal. After all, most school children still read about this
seemingly 'commemorable' event in their history books.

The Irish and the Scandinavians, however, objected to
Spain's proposal, asserting that their own St. Brendan and Lief
Eriksson had arrived on the American continent earlier. The
Africans opposed the proposal, stating understandably that
'colonialism' should not be celebrated in the United Nations.
Speaker after speaker took the floor, supporting or opposing
the proposal. The heated debate enlivened the UN lobbies and
the media publicised the story more than is usual for UN
debates.

The whole question had a sinister but largely unnoticed side
to it: there was hardly any mention of the large-scale genocide
perpetrated in the Americas. Within decades after the
'discovery' of America, whole nations which had thrived there
for centuries had been reduced to nothing. Millions of men,
women and children were massacred. Those who survived
suffered untold misery and deprivation. The conquerors, while
eliminating the indigenous people, also introduced African
slavery on the continent.

History can be re-written. It cannot be undone.

This episode in the UN had a lesson for millions of our fellow human beings: it signalled to the indigenous peoples that five centuries after Columbus, their cause was still not being taken seriously.

The Spanish proposal, however, could not be carried through. It gradually began losing support – even though raised in successive General Assembly sessions – as the underlying irony became apparent to more and more member states.

But the Spanish proposal is not an isolated incident of this kind. Earlier in 1976, when the USA celebrated 200 years of independence, the American Indians and their supporters marched across the continent to remind everyone that, in 1776, it was only thirteen states, constituting the British colonies spread along the Atlantic Coast, which had given birth to the United States of America. Within a century, the USA occupied its present ocean to ocean continental territory. In between, the original Indian nations and communities were crushed, subdued, uprooted or penned in reservations.

More recently, in May 1987, in the presence of the British royal family, a flotilla sailed from England for Australia. The 600 passengers paid thousands of pounds each for the privilege. The event commemorated the departure on 13 May 1787 of a fleet of 11 ships carrying a cargo of convicts to New South Wales where they arrived on 26 January 1788 to give birth to modern Australia. The press in England and Australia reported demonstrations in favour of Aboriginal rights and against the celebration of the 'colonisation' of Australia. The police had to intervene and many arrests were made.

The problems of the indigenous are not limited to the Americas and Australia alone. They exist, in varying degrees, in all continents. Even in countries where the indigenous still constitute a majority, they remain powerless, by and large unheard, misunderstood or simply ignored by their 'civilised' patrons. Their past history is disdained; their way of life scorned; their situation of subjugation unrecognised; their social and economic system unvalued.

Government officials, executives of transnational corporations and officers of development banks have often only a limited knowledge of indigenous societies. Yet the projects these officials authorise – dams, roads, relocations of population – affect irrevocably the peoples who lie in their paths. It is not just a case of ignorance; a basic change of attitude is required.

From the polar reaches of Samiland to the equatorial forests of Brazil, from the deserts of Australia to the mountains of India, the indigenous peoples are united by their common cause. They live in poor and rich countries alike; their cause transcends ideological and national frontiers. It demands urgent humanitarian action.

The purpose of this Report is neither to apportion blame nor to encourage acrimony. It is rather to increase public awareness of indigenous issues so that timely action can be taken at the national and international level to ensure a better future.

The persistent plight of the indigenous people in many parts of the world is an affront to our common humanity. This Report is a tribute to their resilience and to their untiring efforts to be treated equitably.

BACKGROUND

1.   The People

'To an outsider, the vast territory of northern Quebec seems
frozen in time. Populated by hunters, trappers and lumberjacks,
linked to the civilisation far to the south by satellite and twin-
engine planes, it is as unchanging and featureless as the lakes and
streams that furrow its sweeping expanse. This is the home of the
Cree Indian tribe. From time immemorial they have lived off this
land, bounded by the icy waters of James Bay to the west and
Labrador to the east. Only one road penetrates to the heart of the
Cree territory, the little town of Waskaganish, and that's open
only eight weeks a year in the dead of winter, when the
surrounding swamplands are frozen solid.

'But change is coming to the Indian wilderness. Two decades
ago the Hudson's Bay Co. trading post was the only major
building in Waskaganish. In Cree the name means "little house",
to-day it is a thriving community of 1,200 people, with an airport,
a school, an indoor hockey arena. Snowmobiles and rough-terrain
vehicles break the forest silence. Prefab wooden bungalows rise in
a patchwork of newly laid roads; many have satellite dishes
trained on the sky, bringing news and entertainment from the
world outside. "We are accepting the white man's ways too
readily", complains a village elder. The real question, though, is
whether the Indians have a choice. In an eerie reprise of the
19th-century conflicts between the red men and white men, the
Crees are locked in a battle over land in which only the costumes
have changed. Pinstripes and corporate jets have taken the place
of buckskins and arrows; the white trappers and settlers of an
earlier era have given way to a powerful corporate conglomerate
. . . After 15 years of construction and expenditures of $7.9

3

billion, Quebec recently completed a 500-mile-long network of 220 dikes and dams that will send 24,000 megawatts of electricity coursing to cities throughout the province and the northern United States. And that's only the first phase of a project that will generate about $500 million in yearly revenues for the province. Executives at Hydro-Quebec, which owns James Bay Energy, have long touted it as "the project of the century".

'Trouble is, the project of the century has proved to be the headache of the epoch for the Crees. From the time it was announced in the early 1970s, it was clear that the damage to the environment would be profound. Roughly 4,400 square miles of traditional Cree hunting lands have so far been flooded. The dams' reservoirs have caused mercury levels in the soil to rise, contaminating the region's lakes and streams and the fish the Indians depend upon for food. Perreault, chief engineer on the project, says it takes about 20 years for such damage to be undone.

'From a strictly legal point of view, there wasn't much the Crees could do. They held no title to the land, either by treaty or more traditional ownership. Their rights, as they saw them, stemmed from inheritance and the simple fact that they lived there — and had for generations beyond memory. But in Montreal, those claims seemed of small account in the face of the province's energy needs. The massive hydro-electric project, the government declared, would make Quebec the "Texas of the north" . . .

'It was a bruising confrontation. The tribe hired lobbyists and lawyers to press its case. It waged an aggressive and highly sympathetic media campaign. And, in November 1975, seemingly against all odds, it won. Under the James Bay and Northern Quebec Agreement, the Crees were given exclusive hunting, fishing and trapping rights in exchange for extinguishing their aboriginal rights to 400,000 square miles of northern Quebec. A compensation package was worked out worth $168 million (divided between the Crees and the smaller Inuit and Naskapi tribes). They were promised additional state services and, more important, were given rights of self-government involving schools, health services and the administration of local federal and provincial development programs. It was the first comprehensive Indian land-claims settlement in Canada — and it was the first time that Indians had been assigned responsibility for handling

4

their own affairs . . .'

Extract from an article entitled 'Light in the Forest'

Newsweek, June 15, 1987

The location of these events is the Canadian north country, but variants of this scenario can be found in practically every region where indigenous peoples still survive. Their land is seen by outsiders as unoccupied, unclaimed, or unexploited. Their ways of life and systems of agriculture are looked down upon as primitive. At best, indigenous people are expected to welcome assimilation into the economically and socially dominant society; at worst, they are seen as obstacles to the goals of economic development and national security. For their part, indigenous peoples regard themselves as colonised and abused.

In extreme cases these conflicting perspectives have resulted in actual fighting between governments and the indigenous peoples. Where such violence has not taken place, there has still been confrontation. As a consequence, the conflicts between governments and indigenous populations have grown in recent decades to such an extent that their peaceful resolution has become of vital importance to governments and of growing concern to international and non-governmental organisations. The rights of indigenous peoples are beginning to move centre stage.

But who are these peoples, described variously as indigenous, tribal or autochthonous? And why are their lives and societies being threatened? What has happened in the last decades to bring these peoples onto the world stage? What are their demands? And what can the international community and concerned organisations and individuals do to contribute to a just and peaceful solution? These are some of the main questions raised in this Report.

Who are the indigenous?
There is no generally accepted definition of indigenous peoples. However, there are core elements of such a definition which are probably acceptable to all. Nonetheless, the boundary between

what constitutes an indigenous people and an ethnic group is very difficult to draw.

There are four major elements in the definition of indigenous peoples: pre-existence (i.e. the population is descendent of those inhabiting an area prior to the arrival of another population); non-dominance; cultural difference; and self-identification as indigenous.

Other terms are often used to refer to indigenous peoples: autochthonous, ethnic minorities, tribal people, first nations, fourth world. The most undisputed criterion is that indigenous peoples are the descendants of the original inhabitants of a territory taken over through conquest or settlement by aliens. Thus, the native peoples of the Americas or of Australia and New Zealand are indigenous populations. Even in the Americas, however, there are peoples, such as the Metis in Canada and the Chicanos in the western United States, who consider themselves indigenous, despite the persistent controversy over their status. Nevertheless, where there was large-scale European settlement, indigenous populations are relatively easy to identify. In Asia, however, where European occupation was the last in a succession of colonial experiences and where there was no major foreign settlement, the question of indigenousness is more complex. In the Indian sub-continent, for example, the continual migration of peoples into the area during the past thousand years has made the question of antecedence too complex to resolve. There, as in other parts of Asia, indigenous refers to tribal and semi-tribal communities, presently threatened with what is sometimes called 'internal colonisation'.

In Africa, the identification of indigenous peoples has its own specificity arising from the continent's pre-colonial history and its colonial and decolonisation experience. The borders drawn by the colonial powers have in many cases divided peoples, and the consequent severance of traditional ties with the advent of independence has caused considerable suffering. It continues to be the cause of social and political upheavals resulting in the displacement of populations and the flight of refugees. As in Asia, 'indigenous' in Africa refers to threatened, non-dominant peoples. There are certain vulnerable peoples, such as the San (Bushmen) of the Kalahari desert and the Mbuti (Pygmies) of the Central African rain forest whose traditional way of life is threatened by outside forces and whose territories are negatively affected by over-cultivation and the arrival of settlers. In the Sudan and Ethiopia, nomadic peoples are threatened by the settlement policies of governments; many have become refugees.

Although there is no universally accepted definition of indigenous peoples, the United Nations uses a working definition, developed by a Special Rapporteur on the Problem of Discrimination against Indigenous Populations for the United Nations Sub-Commission on Prevention of Discrimination and Protection of Minorities:

> Indigenous populations are composed of the existing descendants of the peoples who inhabited the present territory of a country wholly or partially at the time when persons of a different culture or ethnic origin arrived there from other parts of the world, overcame them and, by conquest, settlement or other means, reduced them to a non-dominant or colonial situation; who today live more in conformity with their particular social, economic and cultural customs and traditions than with the institutions of the country of which they now form a part, under a State structure which incorporates mainly the national, social and cultural characteristics of other segments of the population which are predominant.[1]

The Special Rapporteur included isolated and marginal populations in the definition of 'indigenous':

> Although they have not suffered conquest or colonisation, isolated or marginal groups existing in the country should also be regarded as covered by the notion of 'indigenous populations' for the following reasons: (a) they are descendants of groups which were in the territory of the country at the time when other groups of different cultures or ethnic origins arrived there; (b) precisely because of their isolation from other segments of the country's population they have almost preserved intact the customs and traditions of their ancestors which are similar to those characterised as indigenous; (c) they are, even if only formally, placed under a State structure which incorporates national, social and cultural characteristics alien to their own.[2]

In his final report, a decade later in 1982, the Special

Rapporteur proposed an alternative wording to his original working definition:

> Indigenous communities, peoples and nations are those which, having a historical continuity with pre-invasion and pre-colonial societies that developed on their territories, consider themselves distinct from other sectors of the societies now prevailing in those territories, or parts of them. They form at present non-dominant sectors of society and are determined to preserve, develop and transmit to future generations their ancestral territories, and their ethnic identity, as the basis of their continued existence as peoples, in accordance with their own cultural patterns, social institutions and legal systems.[3]

Significantly, the Special Rapporteur added that the right to define what and who is indigenous belongs to the indigenous peoples themselves. The group can decide on inclusion and exclusion of persons.[4]

The United Nations Working Group on Indigenous Populations has discussed the issue of definition. For all practical purposes, it has deferred the question for the time being and uses the definition and criteria spelled out by the Special Rapporteur.

Although there is overlap in the distinction between indigenous peoples and minorities, in general, indigenous refers to peoples affected by the past 500 years of colonialism. Therefore, minorities within the European continent itself – Basques, Catalans, Romany (Gypsies), migrant workers and others such as the Kurds – are not included in the United Nations' working definition of indigenous populations but rather are considered national minorities, even though the problems they face may be similar to those of the indigenous. On the other hand, the hunting and fishing peoples of the Arctic circle, such as the Sami (Lapps) and Inuit (Eskimos) and their Siberian kin within the USSR consider themselves and are accepted as indigenous.

Indeed, one could characterise indigenous issues and problems as an unresolved part of the legacy of colonialism, the resolution of which has regrettably continued to elude the international system, while national governments remain reluctant to recognise the problems of such populations, if not their very existence.

It is true that, in a few cases of decolonisation, indigenous populations have risen to dominance following independence, and now seek to exclude politically those immigrants brought by the colonisers. This is the case in Fiji and Sri Lanka to-day. Such a result is not the goal in promoting the rights of indigenous peoples.

The question of a definition assumes special importance when it comes to determining who is indigenous and consequently how many indigenous people there are in a given country or region. Certainly, any attempt to adopt a legal definition which may be universally acceptable, must take fully into account the views of the indigenous peoples themselves and not just the views of governments.

An indigenous population, even when it constitutes the majority in a country, possesses all the characteristics of a national minority subjugated by a dominant society. It may share a language or a religion or culture which is different from and often demeaned by the dominant population. On the other hand, an indigenous population may have lost its language, but still maintain its integral identity. Territorial possession or claims characteristically distinguish indigenous populations. Like most minorities, indigenous peoples are often largely excluded from government, administrative and other senior professional jobs. Locked out of the power structures which determine their fate, they are marginal to the mainstream development of the wider society.

The marginalisation of many indigenous peoples is due to the traditional economic activities which they pursue as well as their physical isolation. They are often nomadic or semi-nomadic, and shifting cultivators like the forest-dwelling peoples of Central America or South East Asia. They are herders like the pastoralists of Sahelian Africa or hunters and gatherers like the San (Bushmen) of Southern Africa, the Innu of Labrador or the Indians of the Brazilian Amazon. Many live in remote areas: in the forests, deserts, mountains or tundra. There they have adapted to their environment and are highly dependent upon it.

Indigenous peoples avoid forming overly centralised political institutions and tend to organise at the community level.

9

Background

Decisions are taken only after a consensus is reached by the community. In this respect indigenous communities contrast with most modern states. If the voices of indigenous elders are listened to, it is not because they can call upon forces of coercion, but because they represent a shared knowledge passed on from generation to generation of community life.

For most outsiders, indigenous peoples are often discernible by their dress, language, customs and other external cultural characteristics. But being indigenous is not simply something that is externally manifested. It is a sense of belonging. It is an awareness of having a distinct culture with special characteristics. Indigenous peoples feel themselves to be different from the mainstream societies of the modern state. The conviction of being an indigenous person unites peoples of apparently quite different backgrounds, ranging from the Mayan Indians of Guatemala to the Aborigines of Australia, from the Nordic Sami to the native Hawaiians.

What is shared by most indigenous peoples is a world view which incorporates as its dearest principle a custodial concept of land and natural resources: Mother Earth. Indigenous peoples regard the land or earth as sacred. It is a living entity. As Hayden Burgess, of the World Council of Indigenous Peoples, puts it: 'The earth is the seat of spirituality, the fountain from which our cultures and languages flourish. The earth is our historian, the keeper of events and of the bones of our forefathers.' The Aborigines of Australia see their landscape as peopled by the spirit forms of their ancestors and it can cause them physical pain when drilling rigs bore through rock on sacred sites. When the government of the Philippines began a scheme to dam the rivers of the Cordillera and flood the valleys where the indigenous communities were located, they met fierce resistance. The people protested not only that they would lose their rice terraces and, therefore, their livelihood, but also that their ancestors would be submerged and lost to them forever. Such strong attachments to the land are found in nearly all indigenous societies. It is anathema to them that land can be owned or treated as a commodity to be exploited and abandoned. The land and its natural resources are gifts entrusted to them for safe-keeping and for passing on intact to future generations. There is much to learn from their vision of

10

land, nature and life and the inter-relations between these.

Numbers and locations

Depending on the definition one adopts of indigenous peoples, their number may greatly vary. It is generally agreed that there are an estimated 200 million indigenous people in the world totalling approximately 4 per cent of the global population.[5] They live in all continents, in capitalist and socialist countries, and in rich and poor countries. They cut across ideological and regional frontiers. It is estimated there are some 250,000 Aborigines in Australia, 300,000 Maoris in New Zealand, 60,000 Sami (Lapps) in the Scandinavian countries, 100,000 Inuits (Eskimos) in circumpolar States, some 30 to 80 million (the low figure being governments' estimates; the high figure that of the indigenous themselves) indigenous peoples in Central and South America and 3 to 13 million indigenous people in North America (depending if the Chicanos and Metis are included). In Asia, using a definition of indigenous peoples which includes tribal and nomadic peoples, there are estimated to be some 150 million: in India over 51 million; in China 67 million; in the Philippines 6.5 million; in Bangladesh over one million; in Burma 11 million and in Siberia and the Soviet Far East, some one million; in Oceania, two million. In the broader sense of the definition, several million in Africa could be included.

The indigenous peoples may form a majority of the population, as they do in Guatemala and Bolivia. They may be numerically small, as they are in Brazil or Finland where they account for less than one-tenth of one per cent of the total population. In some countries the indigenous population may run into tens of millions but still only make up a small percentage of the country's people. In India and China, for example, their numbers are of this order but still account for less than 7 per cent of each country's entire population.

By using such large numbers and generalising about their characteristics, there is the danger of suggesting that indigenous peoples are a uniform and homogeneous group. This is far from the case. Even within a single country the indigenous peoples can vary enormously. In China, for example, the recognised 'national minorities', as they are called, are located along the

Southern and North-Western frontiers and include desert herders in the Mongolian region, hill farmers in Tibet and shifting cultivators in the Southern state of Yunnan. While there are certain fundamental commonalities among all indigenous peoples, there are also wide-ranging distinctions. Most importantly there are differences in their relationship with the wider society. The number of totally isolated groups is now small, although there are still several indigenous communities which are fairly cut off from the mainstream, meeting members of the dominant society only for the purpose of trading. The majority of indigenous peoples, however, are now in regular or even continuous contact outside their territories.

Increasingly, indigenous individuals live and work in towns. In the USA and Canada, for example, nearly half of the native peoples live temporarily in cities where they are employed in industry, construction and seasonal employment, while maintaining their ties with their home communities. Even in predominantly rural societies like India, or in Latin America, the indigenous people deprived of land have gravitated to urban centres in search of work. In communities where traditional economies, like reindeer herding among the Sami or hunting and fishing among the Inuit (Eskimos), are still maintained, the main source of income for many is wage labour. In many parts of Asia where indigenous peoples practise shifting cultivation and hold land communally, there are growing numbers of families buying plots of land and becoming settled farmers. Even within indigenous communities there may be enormous variations. In many countries, there are indigenous persons in public office, in the arts and sports, working in factories and cattle ranches, or living in the traditional manner.

The community-based forms of political organisation, as well as economic and social marginalisation, make indigenous people particularly vulnerable to powerful political and economic forces impinging on their societies. Furthermore, the values and ways of life of indigenous peoples are still seen by many governments as inappropriate in the modern world. Their agricultural practices, like herding or shifting cultivation, require extensive access to land. Although some of their methods are regarded as wasteful by governments, in many cases, they still remain the most environmentally sound forms of land usage in fragile arid or tropical lands. Their custodial attitude to land and natural resources are deemed romantic and impractical by governments set on high growth development. In some cases, the beliefs and customs of indigenous peoples are ridiculed as backward and outmoded. In others, a paternalistic 'civilisation' mission prevails. But scientists increasingly recognise that indigenous peoples have a knowledge of traditional medicines, fauna and flora, balanced and unstressful child rearing, farming techniques, and much more which could benefit all of mankind.

At the heart of the indigenous issue is the racist attitude of dominant societies dating back to the invasion by the Spanish Conquistadores who excused the murder of native inhabitants because they were 'less than human'; similar attitudes include that of British settlers who used to organise hunting parties to clear Australia of Aborigines, or of the North American settlers that 'the only good Indian is a dead Indian'. Such attitudes, even though sometimes shrouded are, in varying degrees, still discernible in the relationship between dominant and indigenous societies in many parts of the world.

2. Victims

'The right of conquest has no other foundation than the right of the strongest.'

Jean-Jacques Rousseau, 1762

Many historians still talk about the 'discovery' of Australia or the Americas, as if they were uninhabited planets. Yet there is archaeological evidence which shows that Aborigines have lived in Australia for at least 60,000 years. In South America in 1532, Francisco Pizarro did not encounter a sparsely populated wilderness in the Andes, but a well-ordered, densely populated civilisation stretching from present-day Chile to Colombia, a distance of over 2,000 miles. In Mexico, in 1519, Hernando Cortez led the colonisation of an Aztec kingdom of tens of millions of people. In North America, where France and Britain vied for mastery, there were around 600 Indian nations and communities, some made up of hunting peoples but the majority of settled farmers. American indigenous farmers originated the cultivation of corn, potatoes, beans, squash, pumpkin, cotton and tobacco. Other peoples encountered were skilled hunters and fishermen who had mastered the forests, swamps and seas through inter-relating with the natural world but without destroying it. The European adventurers, gold seekers and entrepreneurs who conquered and subjugated the peoples of the 'New World' continue to be applauded by many as the symbols of a spirited 'Golden Age', but the invasion they heralded distorted or destroyed rich political, economic and cultural traditions.

The invaders rarely tried to understand the native population or coexist with them. Throughout the Americas, Indians were enslaved and sold on the auction block. They were pushed out of their territories as the frontiers moved. Power struggles between kingdoms on the European continent were duplicated in their colonies, setting tribe against tribe. In Australia, land was fenced off and the Aborigines, who had hitherto roamed freely, were treated as trespassers. The demographic statistics are a grim reminder of the horrors attendant upon European 'discovery' rather than its glories. The population of the Aztec empire was reduced in little over a century from 30 million to 10 million. In Australia the Aboriginal population of 300,000 on the eve of colonisation 1788 had been reduced to about 60,000 a century later. The Spanish killed or deported every Carib Indian on the island of Hispaniola (Haiti) following their arrival, repopulating the island with African slaves. The Chamorro peoples of the Marianas Islands in the Pacific were reduced from over 70,000 to 1,600 in less than 60 years, as a result of a programme of forced relocation by the Spanish colonial authorities. In Tasmania, a favoured Sunday sport was native-hunting.

The violence used by the Europeans against the indigenous peoples inhabiting the colonised territories is well chronicled. Spanish officials and British settlers, fearful of rebellion by a numerically stronger native population, and needing cheap land and labour to produce the wealth they sought, uprooted the people from their territories. In North America, the policy of indiscriminate killing of Indian men, women and children was often sanctioned at the highest levels. Indians, the Kansas newspaper *Weekly Leader* in the USA commented in 1867, were 'a set of miserable, dirty, louse-infected, gut-eating skunks as the Lord permitted to live. Their immediate and final extermination all men should pray for.' The sentiment that the native people were sub-human and inferior was common among the European invaders.

Racist attitudes of this kind do not alone account for the destruction of so many indigenous peoples, although what would be considered genocide today was accepted as an integral part of colonial policy. Perhaps as deadly as the gun were the epidemic diseases which ran rampant as the indigenous became refugees or enslaved. Influenza, tuberculosis, smallpox and measles decimated entire native communities. Over the long term, the continual annexation of land by the growing settler population itself struck a severe blow because it deprived indigenous people of the means of survival. The practice of the

15

European monarchs was to allocate vast tracts of land as rewards to their administrators and contractors in the colonies. In some areas the indigenous population felt no difference and continued to work the land as before, often paying tribute in kind. But, as time passed, they learned that the land was claimed by someone else, and that their produce and even their labour was now at his disposal. As the Europeans took over the land, the indigenous inhabitants became increasingly dispossessed and dependent.

In North America, the governments of Britain and later the USA and Canada signed over 300 treaties with Indian nations, including promises of inalienable reserve lands, many of which were subsequently broken. The Maoris in New Zealand signed the Treaty of Waitangi in 1840 by which they ceded sovereignty in exchange for exclusive and undisturbed land rights. But within a few years, the British Crown forcibly purchased half of the total guaranteed area, about 30 million acres, and by successive acts of Parliament, much of the rest has also been wrested from the hands of the Maoris. Today they own only about four per cent of New Zealand territory. The Maoris, as well as North American Indians, now insist on their treaty rights, and demand that those treaties be considered legitimate international agreements.

The present situation of indigenous peoples is rooted in their colonial past. If they are largely landless, underprivileged and discriminated against, it is because of the relationship of conqueror and conquered which was established during the early years of colonial contact. A higher proportion of indigenous peoples in all countries today remain unemployed than in society as a whole. Even when employed, they are concentrated in unskilled and low paid jobs. In the USA, half the Indians living on reservations have no work.[1] In Australia the Aboriginal unemployment rate is more than seven times that for the country as a whole.[2] In New Zealand one in seven Maoris is unemployed while the figure is only one in 30 for the rest of the population.[3] Their incomes are lower than those of the rest of society. In the USA, for example, the per capita income of Indians is significantly lower than that of other disadvantaged groups and is only half the national average.

In Africa, Asia and Latin America, indigenous people are the poorest of the poor. In the Brazilian and Peruvian Amazon, in Eastern Bolivia and in Paraguay, there are cases of Indians working as virtual slaves as debt-bonded labourers.[4] They are pressured by local landowners and entrepreneurs into taking a loan and are charged high interest. They pay the debt with labour. The landowner advances money to buy tools and food, and when the reckoning is made at the end of the month, the debt remains. There is no escape. Any attempt to evade the debt can result in imprisonment or, as has happened in some places, murder. Such practice is illegal universally, but the criminals are rarely prosecuted when their victims are indigenous.

In India, many of the workers hired to build the stadiums, hotels and roads for the Asian Games in 1982 were people trapped in precisely this cycle of debt by employment agents. The Government of India's *Report of the Commission for Scheduled Castes and Scheduled Tribes* in 1981 acknowledged the vulnerability of the indigenous to this form of exploitation, and stated that the majority of these communities survived below the poverty line and were among the poorest 30 per cent of the country's population.

Indigenous people also suffer comparatively poor health. In the rich countries the differences are marked. In the USA, for example, malnutrition, as well as obesity, are higher among Indians than any other group; Native Americans are eight times more likely to contract tuberculosis than other US citizens.[5] In Australia, the average life span of an Aboriginal is about 20 years less than that of a White.[6] High infant mortality largely accounts for the disparity. In Queensland, Australia, a 1983 medical report found that the death rate from infectious diseases was nine times higher in Aboriginal reserves than elsewhere in the state.[7] Inadequate government health care has led Aboriginal people to set up their own medical services. In Canada and the USA, Indian infant mortality is twice that of other North Americans.[8]

In Latin America, where health care systems are poor in any case, the indigenous population generally fares worse than other rural poor. The Mayan Indians of Guatemala have a life expectancy 11 years shorter than the dominant Euro–American minority and similar figures apply to the highland Indians of Bolivia and Peru.[9]

Background

The high mortality rate among the indigenous is often attributed to their inability or unwillingness to take part in modern health care programmes. However, their poor health is generally a symptom of their impoverished and deprived position in society. Primary health care often does not extend to remote communities. Sometimes, among relatively isolated indigenous communities, dramatic rises in mortality can occur because of contact with outsiders. In Brazil, it is estimated that 87 Indian groups this century have become extinct as a consequence of epidemic diseases.[10] In Venezuela measles and whooping cough epidemics have caused mortality rates of up to 30 per cent in some groups of Yanomami.[11] The health conditions of the indigenous are often given lower priority by governments than other major social and economic problems. In Thailand, for example, there were no official health visits to the indigenous villages until 1985, and medical care tends to be dispensed by local priests or resident shamans who are ill-equipped to deal with epidemics.

The perpetuation of the underprivileged position of most indigenous peoples has been ensured by the low priority accorded to their education by governments. This is reflected in the low investment in rural, and particularly, indigenous education. For instance, the provision of schooling of any kind by governments among the forest-dwelling peoples of Asia and Amazonia is almost non-existent. Even among more accessible and settled indigenous communities, the educational facilities are of a low quality. The result is that almost everywhere the indigenous are the worst educated group in society. According to the Government of India, the literacy rate is 11 per cent for 'scheduled tribes' but 30 per cent for the total population.[12] In the USA, the drop-out rate among Indian children is twice the national average. In Australia, few Aboriginal people reach secondary school, let alone study for degrees or professional qualifications. This is not to say that there have not emerged exceptional scholars, intellectuals, artists and professionals from indigenous communities, but more often this has been in spite of the educational system rather than because of it. One reason for the drop-out rate among the indigenous who do have access to schooling is language alienation, and even where bilingual education programmes exist, they are often only transitional and the content is alien and value-laden.

In any case, government schools generally pursue an educational programme which is either scornful of indigenous values, histories and traditions or simply omits any reference to them. The medium of instruction is usually the language of the dominant society and not that of the indigenous community. Teachers recruited into indigenous schools often consider it a punishment posting and maintain strong prejudices against the societies they educate. The result is tragic for the children. They are taught that the culture of their parents is backward, and that they will never properly be accepted by the wider society. They end up alienated and demoralised, shorn of their cultural roots yet unable to take a place in the non-indigenous world.

Probably most harmful of all to indigenous communities have not been government schools, but evangelising religious movements such as the Summer Institute of Linguistics or the New Tribes Mission and various Christian sects. These well-funded fundamentalist missions, as well as a great number of other mainstream foreign missions, have penetrated many isolated communities, from Papua New Guinea to Amazonia. They impose their own view of the world and win some of the people over through the provision of material assistance and health care which is not forthcoming from governments. In some countries, these missions have caused such conflict within indigenous communities that they have been expelled, but their work elsewhere remains undiminished.[13] Investigations by indigenous and other non-governmental organisations into the operations of the Summer Institute of Linguistics led to a resolution by the Organisation of American States calling on its members to expel these missionaries. However, no country has as yet done so.

The laws and constitutions of most countries provide for the protection of the indigenous peoples located on their territories. There are no legal obstacles to indigenous peoples attaining high office. In New Zealand, for example, the post of Governor-General is currently occupied by a Maori. In Brazil in 1983, a Xavante Indian was elected federal deputy for Rio de Janeiro. Some countries even take positive measures in favour of indigenous peoples. In India, 40 of the 542 seats in the national parliament and about eight per cent of seats in the state legislatures are reserved for 'members of scheduled tribes'.

Nonetheless, such examples of positive government action have not improved the overall political and legal position of the majority of indigenous peoples. They are effectively disenfranchised in many countries and cannot hope to influence national policy through the ballot box without significant support from other sectors. Where individuals from indigenous communities win political power, they are often co-opted into the ruling party and cease to represent the interests of their community. In the USA, the official Tribal Councils established in 1934 by the government to administer the Indian reservations have often been accused of being corrupt, unrepresentative of the community and in league with outside business interests. In Queensland, Australia, Aborigines living on reserves can even be denied a vote in local elections. The government agencies set up to protect the rights of the indigenous often do little more than facilitate the exploitation of their land. In the Philippines, the main office protecting indigenous peoples (PANAMIN) – disbanded in 1985 – had no representative of the peoples concerned, and its head, like most members of the board, was a wealthy businessman owning mining and logging companies with direct interests in indigenous resources. In Brazil, the National Indian Foundation (FUNAI) is responsible to the Ministry of the Interior, and notwithstanding some dedicated pro-Indian staff, has served the development and security goals of the government, rather than those of the country's vulnerable indigenous peoples. As a consequence FUNAI has been unable fully to protect indigenous lands from invasion by settlers and speculators.

The police often abuse the indigenous. The courts, with their overwhelmingly non-indigenous judges and juries, are not free of prejudice. In Victoria, Australia, Aboriginal people are 45 times more likely to go to prison than Whites; in the Northern Territory 90 per cent of all arrests are of Aborigines.[14] In the US states of Alaska, Arizona and South Dakota, the indigenous Indians, less than 10% of the population, account for 60% of the prison population. In some Latin American countries, all poor people face abuse by officials and the police, but Indians are particularly targeted.

When the largely self-governing and economically self-reliant societies of indigenous peoples are thrown into the mainstream, they undergo a major transformation. Unable to maintain their independence, they are forced to accept work on the bottom rung of the social ladder. Those who do not find work often drift into a marginalised world of petty crime, alcoholism and prostitution. Other manifestations of social and cultural trauma are reflected in disrupted family life and high suicide rates. Once proud and independent people are reduced to the poorest of the poor. Their new habitats are not the forests, prairies and outback, but the slums, fringe camps and shanty towns. To be 'integrated' in this negative way into the dominant society is nothing short of ethnocide; which means that a people are denied their right to enjoy, develop and disseminate their own culture and language. This has been the fate of many millions of indigenous peoples since colonisation began and today remains a threat to millions more.

Governments, international agencies, non-governmental organisations and corporations, as well as individuals, all have a role in changing this situation by reversing the course of history which continues to subject indigenous peoples to such injustice.

One of the first features that must be eliminated is the celebration of 'discovery'. Indeed, 1992, the 500-year anniversary of Columbus reaching America, should be declared International Year for Indigenous Peoples. National histories throughout the world must be revised, not only for the benefit of the indigenous, but also for the general population, who presently learn false history, thereby perpetuating racism, intolerance, and support for inhuman policies. At the international level, the United Nations Educational, Scientific and Cultural Organisation (UNESCO) could assure that technical means are directed toward revising national histories. UNESCO, despite its achievements in raising the banner of the 'right to be different' and encouraging cultural diversity, has not encouraged research by the indigenous. Nor do programmes exist for developing technical skills among the indigenous in order to enable them to be their own archaeologists, linguists, demographers, and other specialists.

In the areas of health, education and social welfare, governments must provide similar services for the indigenous, as they do for the rest of the population. Governments do not presently make requests of the World Health Organisation (WHO) to achieve such a goal. Donor governments do not insist that funding priorities include indigenous communities. Indeed, the largest donors to financial institutions, such as the World Bank, have hardly favoured loans and grants for social services. Inside the rich countries, social services are also shrinking, and the indigenous, being among the poorest, are hurt the most. Authentic bilingual, bicultural education must be implemented in every country. Presently, it does not even exist in principle – let alone actual policy – in most countries.

Governments can control and restrain missionaries from their present free-wheeling activities in indigenous communities. The churches themselves should play a role in halting ethnocidal practices.

Thus far, it has been the indigenous themselves who have organised to better wage their fight for survival, and they have accomplished much since they took the decision to raise their issues at the international level. They insist on being fully involved in all decisions that affect their communities and futures, and will settle for no less.

3. Invasions

'We punish murders and massacres among private persons. What do we do respecting wars, and the glorious crime of murdering whole nations?'

Seneca the Younger, 59 A.D.

Since the Second World War the number of incursions into indigenous peoples' lands has escalated worldwide. Once thought of as barren wastelands of little economic and political value, indigenous territories have now been identified as areas of vital national and even international importance. The last frontiers of forest, desert, mountain and tundra are now being opened up like so many pearl oysters. The riches are torn out, the land taken over and the ideological conflicts between alien powers and the nationalism of governments brought in to bloody the people. The impact of this exploitation is far reaching. With no untroubled or uncoveted regions to retreat to, the native inhabitants have been forced to accept these invasions reluctantly, or else fight back. Where there has been acceptance by them of national development on their land, there has also been forced assimilation and degradation of their way of life; where there has been resistance, there has sometimes followed violent conflict and loss of life.

Yet these incursions also have another result. They have stimulated the formation of new organisations of indigenous peoples, and strategies of national and international political action. These organisations have made sustained efforts to force the international community to take note of their situation and the informed general public to become more aware of the world-wide nature of the indigenous peoples' movement.

But what are the causes of these recent invasions of indigenous peoples' lands? What kind of political and economic changes have taken place to generate outside interest

23

in the marginal homelands of indigenous peoples? And why are these threatened peoples now uniting to confront the invasions of their territories?

One of the prime interests in indigenous peoples' land is economic. Since the 1950s the rich countries have experienced extensive economic growth and a boom in demand for consumer goods. The gross world product of goods and services and the consumption of energy have quadrupled since the Second World War. Stimulated also by the expansion in the manufacture of armaments and related military technology, and several regional wars, this explosion in demand and production has boosted a world-wide search for raw materials. Traditional sources became insufficient to satisfy the vastly expanded demand, and the major mining companies – mostly based in the rich countries – began to look for new areas of untapped natural resources.

During the 1950s and 1960s the search for new resources led North American companies to the reservations and traditional territories of indigenous populations in Canada and the US. In the rich countries, many of the unexploited resources are to be found on land formerly believed to be valueless and therefore still held by indigenous peoples. In the United States of America, for example, about 40 per cent of all uranium deposits and 15 per cent of surface-minable coal are located on Indian reserves. The opportunities for profitable exploitation of the natural resources of these areas were seized upon by the mining companies. In the late 1950s, for example, Peabody Coal, Utah International and other US multinational companies negotiated leases on land from the government-run Bureau of Indian Affairs, to mine coal on the Navajo reservation. The royalties paid to the Navajos were fixed at a low rate with no allowance made for any increase in the market value of coal. In 1981, therefore, the Navajos only received around 25 cents a ton in royalties, whereas the market price was in the region of US $70 a ton.[1]

In Australia, Aboriginal land was also found to contain important mineral reserves. In the 1950s some of the world's largest bauxite deposits were discovered in Northern Queensland. Rio Tinto Zinc and Kaiser Aluminium managed to obtain a lease on 2,000 square miles of Aboriginal land at the rate of £2 a square mile instead of the £300 or more a square mile for equivalent non-Aboriginal land.[2] This pattern of exploitation was repeated in many of the developed nations. The Inuit of Alaska, the Dene people of Northern Canada, the Aboriginal peoples of Australia, the Oglala Sioux and other Indian nations in the United States of America and many other indigenous peoples in the rich countries have been pushed off their land during the last three decades to make way for oil and mining companies.

The story is a similar one for indigenous peoples in other parts of the world. Where there is mineral wealth, the indigenous inhabitants are removed. In Amazonia, indigenous groups have been pushed aside to make way for mining companies. About 45 per cent of the mineral production of India and one-third of its known reserves are on indigenous lands in the state of Bihar. Yet the native inhabitants benefit little from the wealth and employment generated in the region.[3]

As the competition for the control and extraction of resources has intensified, the search has extended to areas of low population density. In the mid-1960s, Brazil's Amazon region was opened up to prospectors and cattle ranchers, and in the same period, the forests throughout South and South East Asia began to face pressure by logging companies.

Just as the desert and semi-desert regions left to the Aborigines and North American Indian nations were found to contain important deposits of coal, uranium, bauxite and other minerals, so the forests which are the home of at least one million indigenous people in Amazonia and Central America and perhaps as many as 40 million in Asia, were recognised as sources of exportable wealth.

The growth in the demand for timber this century, and particularly since mid-century, has been truly dramatic. At present, the global consumption of wood is 3,000 million cubic metres a year and is expected to rise to 4,000 million cubic metres by the year 2000. In 1900 timber consumption was about a quarter of this figure. In the developed countries there has been a boom particularly in the consumption of hardwoods, from 4 million cubic metres in 1950 to 70 million cubic metres in 1980, a 16-fold increase. Japan, the major market for Asian hardwoods, saw its consumption of wood rocket many-fold

25

between 1950 and 1974.[4] This apparently insatiable and ever growing demand, particularly of the rich nations, for the world's natural resources has spurred a global search by governments, multinationals and entrepreneurs. Many of these resources are exploited in 'frontier' lands occupied by indigenous peoples.

Other pressures have also acted to draw mainstream society onto indigenous peoples' land. In the developing countries, the process of industrialisation and urbanisation has accelerated rapidly in the last 30 years. Leaps in population have occurred in all major cities in the Third World. The population of Sao Paulo in Brazil, for example, has grown from a few hundred thousand at the turn of the century to 16 million; by the year 2000 the number is expected to be 25 million. The extractive, manufacturing, construction and basic service industries in these countries have also grown with great rapidity. Jamshedpur in India – in the 1920s a small town in Bihar – has become within two generations a sprawling, polluted and congested city with more than one million inhabitants and some of the country's largest industries. In Amazonia, entire towns have been built to serve new industry where two decades ago there was only forest.

The surge in industrialisation and urbanisation on indigenous peoples' traditional land, and more generally in developing countries, has compelled the development of energy resources by governments. Since the 1960s, many poor countries, mainly in response to industrial needs and encouraged by the availability of financial support from the multilateral development banks, have invested in hydro-power. Indigenous peoples were the first victims of the rush of large dams built in the USA. Globally, they continue to form a large proportion of the population displaced by such schemes. It is not difficult to see why governments choose indigenous peoples' land for the generation of hydro-electric power. The territories of indigenous peoples, consisting of river valleys of comparatively low population density, are generally physically suited to dam construction. Indigenous people are politically marginal and therefore unable to protest effectively. Most importantly, they often do not have clear ownership rights in the modern sense to the land designated for hydro-electric development, so governments are not obliged to provide expensive compensation. Even when they do have recognised rights, legislation may be enacted to disenfranchise them.

Furthermore, since mid-century the world's population has doubled to some 5 billion and this fact alone accounts for strong outside pressures on indigenous territories. The increase has been the greatest in the poor countries, and the excess rural population has either drifted into the towns in search of work or moved to marginal hill and forest lands. Rural unemployment and landlessness have been exacerbated by the post-war shift in agricultural production. In both rich and poor countries the overall trend has been towards land concentration and agribusiness. Family farms growing food for domestic consumption have given way to large, highly mechanised estates producing cash crops for the export market. Countless self-sufficient farmers have seen their livelihoods destroyed by this process.

Indigenous peoples have been affected by the growing landlessness of non-indigenous agriculturalists. They have faced competition for their better quality land and often lost it. In Thailand, for example, virtually all the lower valleys in the north-western hill region, once exclusively farmed communally, are now occupied by farmers who came in from elsewhere. Increasingly, landless peasants are moving higher up the hills and registering their ownership of land with the government. The natives, with only a tradition of communal use of the land and no title of collective or individual ownership, are displaced.

Where governments have had political confrontations with landless peasants, such as in the north-east of Brazil, they have devised colonisation programmes. The impoverished peasants of the region demanded a radical redistribution of land in the 1960s, and part of the government strategy to defuse the unrest was to offer pioneer colonists plots of land in Amazonia. The prospect of owning a large piece of land attracted many poor, landless peasants into the colonisation schemes. The areas designated for colonisation often impinged upon Indian territory, and conflicts between these two disadvantaged groups in Brazil have become a regular feature of those areas.

There are also political, as well as economic, reasons for the invasion of indigenous peoples' territories. Immense changes in international relations have taken place since the Second World War. Until then the indigenous peoples often retained some degree of informal political and economic autonomy. In many instances this was more by default than for any other reason. Indigenous people were often relatively isolated and the extraction of resources from their land was not on a scale sufficient to threaten their survival.

Dramatic changes came about following the European withdrawal from their colonies after the Second World War. In 1945 there were 51 independent States; today these have more than tripled. Most of these newly independent countries are in Africa, Asia and the Pacific and are not linguistically, culturally or ethnically homogeneous. There are, for example, 400 different ethnic groups in Nigeria, 400 recognised 'scheduled tribes' in India, and 300 linguistic groups in Indonesia. One of the most difficult problems faced by the newly independent nations has been to achieve the unity of their disparate populations and to encourage a sense of national identity. In Asia, for example, the new states of Bangladesh, Burma, India and Indonesia have assiduously guarded the frontiers established by the colonial powers and refused to recognise the demands for self-determination of the indigenous peoples they have incorporated.[5] In fact, they have actively sought to repress movements for autonomy. Military operations, under the guise of national security, in the Chittagong Hill Tracts of Bangladesh, in Naga and Mizo lands in north-east India, in the South Moluccas and West Papua in Indonesia, and in the homelands of Karen, Kachin and other hill people in Burma resemble the methods of colonial control of the past.

Governments and the international community as a whole have been reluctant to renegotiate international frontiers or discuss questions of secession. Instead, the territorial integrity of the states formed after the European withdrawal has been protected. The results of this tragic dilemma can be seen in different parts of the world. Secessionist struggles, sometimes intermittent, often little reported internationally, but nevertheless costly in human life, are being fought in many countries around the world. A serious side-effect is the displacement of hundreds of thousands of people, creating the intractable problem of refugees.

The East–West confrontation has also brought indigenous peoples into the international arena and led to further incursions onto their land. Many of the areas once thought of as unstrategic are now deemed vital to the defence of the superpowers and their allies. US and French military bases and nuclear tests, for example, are reported to have disrupted the lives of the native inhabitants of the Pacific, provoking a vigorous popular movement for demilitarisation in the region. Hunting and gathering peoples in the Philippines have been removed from their territories to make way for the US air and naval bases. In Labrador in Canada, the caribou-hunting Innu Indian people are being excluded from their traditional territories because the area is a NATO site for supersonic aircraft and weapons testing. There is evidence that the exploding of atomic bombs by Britain in the 1950s was carried out over Aboriginal land in Australia with scant concern for the protection and welfare of the inhabitants. The US has fired its intercontinental ballistic missiles into the Kwajalein Atoll in the Pacific causing long-term damage to the surrounding eco-system and affecting the peoples dependent on it. In the name of national security, countless indigenous peoples have had to give up their homes and livelihoods, if they have not lost their lives. Indians in the South West of the USA are reported to have suffered serious health problems due to nuclear tests in or around their territories.

Because indigenous peoples are ethnically different from the majority, they are often regarded with suspicion by the dominant society. If they live on and across borders – as is often the case in Africa, Asia and Latin America – they may be recruited by distant protagonists creating local conflict by proxy. The hill tribes of Indo-China, to their cost, were embroiled by both sides during the war in the 1960s and 1970s. Today there is hardly a part of the globe unaffected by preparations for war, and among those already paying the highest price are the indigenous peoples.

The political and economic changes which have taken place in the last three decades have impinged upon the lives of formerly comparatively isolated indigenous peoples. However, other factors have contributed to the awakening of indigenous consciousness and their present world-wide movement. The process of decolonisation itself raised expectations among many indigenous peoples that full independence could be achieved. Untutored in international affairs, however, they were unable to raise sufficient support among their own people or find strong allies to support their cause. But these indigenous peoples do claim that the international law elaborated since 1945 guarantees their right of self-determination.

Increasingly, the indigenous are making demands for self-management not only in the poor but also in the rich countries. In the USA, intensified threats of dispossession in the 1950s, including a government plan to terminate Indian status completely, led to peaceful protest and civil disobedience to obtain political concessions from the government. They, like the Aboriginal people in Australia and the Maoris in New Zealand, have been successful in drawing public attention to their condition and forcing the question of land rights onto the political agenda.

In South and Central America there has been a similar growth of indigenous peoples' organisations. The large-scale development projects in Amazonia, with their disruptive effects on forest-dwelling Indians, have served to galvanise small community-based organisations. Traditionally, the Amazonian Indian population consists of small, relatively independent communities and these have not had any strong reasons to unite. The national development programmes in the Amazonian regions of Peru, Brazil and Ecuador which began in the 1960s have changed this situation. Their impact has been widespread and has introduced a common problem for the indigenous peoples; Amazonian development has acted as a catalyst for the regional movement of indigenous peoples.

The incursions into their lands are made in the name of economic development and national security. Yet they generally provide neither improvements in the material well-being of indigenous peoples nor in their physical and psychological security. Instead national development, as it is presently imposed, destroys many indigenous communities while benefiting only a few entrepreneurs.

4. Indigenous Movements and Aspirations

'An aspiration is a joy forever, a possession as solid as a landed estate.'

Robert Louis Stevenson, 1881

International organisations, governments and other concerned bodies have begun to consider seriously the demands of indigenous peoples. Multilateral development banks and transnational corporations, too, are gradually beginning to catch up. But what are the aspirations of the indigenous peoples? What are their main demands and what methods are they adopting to achieve their goals?

Although there is a high level of indigenous consensus in identifying issues, there is, of course, no uniformity among the indigenous peoples, just as there is no uniformity among states. Indigenous peoples range from those who function within the dominant society (even though disadvantaged) to those who are isolated and maintain few links with the mainstream. There are those who subsist as hunters and gatherers. There are others who earn high salaries as professional workers in urban centres. There are those who have retained or revived their traditional customs and culture – their language, dress, dance, close relationship with the land and nature, and ceremonies – and those who have adopted Western customs and styles of life. Outlooks and aspirations, therefore, are not necessarily the same within all indigenous communities.

Their colonial and national experiences also differ widely. The social and economic systems imposed by the Spanish and Portuguese in South and Central America are different from that experienced by those under British and French rule in North America. Nor are the present-day national political systems in which indigenous peoples live all alike. The democratic freedoms theoretically available to Aborigines in

31

Australia, for example, are not guaranteed to forest Indians by the military regime of President Stroessner in Paraguay. Finally, the economies of the different nations vary greatly. The United States of America, with its enormous financial resources, is not under the same pressures as, for example, Honduras, to develop its forests, potential agricultural land, minerals and other natural resources. It may not be excused, but it can be more readily understood, how Honduras in its search for shortcuts to economic development harms its indigenous population. But the similar attitudes which exist in countries such as Canada, Sweden or the USA are more difficult to rationalise.

An international movement of indigenous peoples has steadily developed to defend and promote their interests in a concerted manner. The lead came from the Americas, and although indigenous peoples in Africa and Asia have been less active at regional or international levels, there is increasing awareness of the imperative need to participate. Bound together in defence of a common cause, further progress by indigenous peoples in all parts of the world in the direction of a strong international lobby seems certain.

In the early 1970s, indigenous peoples of the Americas, the Arctic, and South Pacific formed networks, despite the differences in their colonial and national situations and individual circumstances. Since then, hundreds of indigenous peoples' organisations, representing communities of less than a few dozen households to territories with populations of several million, have been founded. These organisations have stretched out from their local communities and interests to meet and support one another.

The first international initiative arose out of the frustration experienced by the North American-based American Indian Movement (AIM) in its attempts to have the Indian treaties with the United States and Canada recognised and the violations redressed. In 1974, AIM called a meeting of grassroots indigenous peoples from all over the Western Hemisphere and the Pacific. Over 5,000 persons, representing hundreds of local organisations, participated and founded the International Indian Treaty Council. The new organisation immediately petitioned for non-governmental status in the

Economic and Social Council of the United Nations (ECOSOC), and established offices in New York. Consultative status in ECOSOC was granted in early 1977, which set a precedent for other federations of indigenous peoples and organisations to apply for the same status.[1]

In 1975, the National Indian Brotherhood of Canada also established an international arm and began to reach out to indigenous organisations in the Americas, the Arctic and the Pacific, and to the well organised Sami people of Scandinavia. They established the World Council of Indigenous Peoples (WCIP),[2] and also applied for and received consultative status in ECOSOC in 1979. At its 1984 conference in Panama, nearly 300 indigenous delegates from 23 different countries participated.

About 35 million indigenous peoples are thereby directly and indirectly linked through these two federations.

By 1987, eight more organisations representing indigenous peoples had received consultative status in ECOSOC – some regional, such as the South American Indian Council (CISA), the National Aborigine and Islander Services Secretariat, and the Inuit Circumpolar Conference, and some with more sectoral or legal inclinations, such as the Indian Law Resource Center in Washington D.C., the Four Directions Council, the National Indian Youth Council (USA), and the Indigenous World Association. In 1987 the Grand Council of the Cree (Quebec) became the first indigenous nation to achieve its own status in ECOSOC as a non-governmental organisation.

In addition, a number of organisations already concerned about indigenous peoples have supported their international initiatives. Survival International, Minority Rights Group, and the Anti-Slavery Society of Great Britain, for example, have participated actively in international forums concerned with the protection of indigenous peoples. Other non-governmental organisations and religious groupings, such as the World Council of Churches, have developed special sections on indigenous issues. And many others, such as Amnesty International, have put indigenous concerns high on their agendas.

Indigenous peoples' organisations have had enormous difficulties in establishing themselves. In Brazil, for example,

Background

the Union of Indian Nations (UNI) – the main Indian organisation – is underfunded, understaffed and dependent upon meagre church and non-governmental financial support. Organisers have constituencies spread throughout a tropical rain forest the size of France and, inevitably, liaison between them and their semi-nomadic supporters is difficult. Furthermore, there are often long-standing disputes among neighbouring indigenous peoples. The new generation of activists has tried to overcome these. Also, the drastic and universal impact of many national development projects has brought traditionally hostile groups together around a common programme of protest and resistance. For example, when the government of the Philippines began its dam-building project in the Cordillera, the threatened indigenous communities buried their differences and united in their traditional *bodong* or peace pact.

Activity by indigenous peoples' organisations at the international level is relatively new and recent. There are still many peoples who remain uninformed about the activities undertaken on their behalf. In Asia, for example, there are still very few political organisations to defend the interests of indigenous communities. On the other hand, bodies such as the World Council of Indigenous Peoples or the International Indian Treaty Council, formed more than a decade ago, already have enormous experience in advocacy at national and international levels and can count on skilled professional assistance, even though they have to rely mostly on voluntary staff due to inadequate financial support.

Despite the diversity and geographical spread of indigenous populations, there is an increasingly unified approach by them in terms of aspirations and goals. However, differences in terms of perceptions and leadership create difficulties in achieving the cooperation required to pursue common goals at the global level.

In practical terms, there is a variation in the kinds of strategy adopted even in pursuit of their aims at the national level. In the USA, native Americans have had some success in the courts and used litigation and negotiation to recover or be compensated for land seized in the past, or to obtain improved royalties from mining companies. Other groups have used political protest, demonstrations and acts of civil disobedience to raise public awareness of their causes. The Aborigines of Australia acquired national and international publicity when they established a tent embassy in the grounds of Parliament House in Canberra in 1972. Hundreds of indigenous peoples' organisations have now presented their cases to the United Nations Commission on Human Rights and its subsidiary organs in an attempt to attract the interest and involvement of the international community and to develop international protective measures. In the course of these non-violent actions, indigenous peoples have won the support of trade unions, churches and liberal opinion, although the vast majority of the public remains ignorant of indigenous demands and the extent of their plight and suffering.

In India the indigenous peoples of Bihar formed their own political party and put up candidates for the state and national legislatures. The Jharkhand Party at its height in the 1950s held over 30 seats in the State Assembly and became a major opposition party. Similarly, the Indians of Bolivia formed a political party in the 1950s. In Brazil indigenous peoples stood for state and federal seats in the 1986 elections, having experienced, as was mentioned earlier, the successful election in 1983 of a Xavante Indian as deputy for Rio de Janeiro. In Nicaragua, a Miskito Indian was elected to the National Assembly in 1984.

But legal and peaceful strategies have not always been adopted by indigenous peoples. More often than not, this is because such channels are closed or else, in the past, have not served to advance their interests. In desperation, some indigenous peoples have taken up arms in the past 30 years. Currently, fighting is taking place in, amongst other countries, Bangladesh, Burma, Guatemala, Indonesia, Peru and the Philippines. In Burma, the Karen have been fighting the government since 1948. In Indonesia's province of Irian Jaya, West Papuan guerillas have been active since the 1960s, and in Bangladesh the Shanti Bahini, the local armed opposition, has been operational for more than a decade. In Peru, the impoverished Ayacucho province is aflame with guerilla war being fought by Quechua Indians.

The demands of indigenous peoples are of two main kinds:

35

those which are essentially political and may be considered as demands for self-determination, and those which are economic and cultural and which may be classified under land rights. There are, of course, a great many other demands being made by indigenous peoples, but they can for the most part be subsumed under these two categories.

The meanings given to the term self-determination by different indigenous peoples' organisations cover a wide spectrum.

The World Council of Indigenous Peoples' Declaration of Principles drafted in 1984 states:

> All indigenous nations have the right of self-determination. By virtue of this right they may freely determine their political status and freely pursue their economic, social, religious and cultural development.

This statement on self-determination thus claims for indigenous peoples the rights accorded to all peoples by the UN's International Covenants on Civil and Political Rights and on Economic, Social and Cultural Rights. It is, of course, a controversial claim because it challenges the absolute sovereignty of nation states.

In fact, few indigenous peoples' organisations seek full political independence. The Kanaks in New Caledonia, still living under what they regard as French colonial rule, want an independent country like their Melanesian neighbours in Papua New Guinea or Vanuatu. The West Papuan guerilla force – the Free Papua Movement (OPM) – is demanding independence from Indonesia, whose occupation it considers illegal. But even where there has been fierce fighting between indigenous peoples and governments, it has not necessarily been because the former seek independence. In Burma, the Karen and other indigenous peoples are united in fighting for self-governing autonomous territories, but within a federated union. The Karen – a people with a population of some four to five million – have had *de facto* control over their territory (Kowthoolei), a civilian government and an army since 1948.

The demands of the hill people in the Chittagong Hill Tracts are for an end to occupation of their lands by outsiders, and political autonomy within the state of Bangladesh. The hill people are not asking for independence, but for some constitutional arrangements for the preservation of their cultures and identities, control over the administration of their homeland, and their own legislature.

In some places indigenous peoples are not demanding even such formal political changes. By 'self-determination' they often mean that they want control over the day-to-day running of their lives, or autonomy, as cities and towns have in terms of municipal laws and practices. Most, however, are demanding that autonomy be enshrined in law, and protected by international agreement and machinery.

Indigenous peoples have highly developed political, legal and social systems which have worked successfully for centuries, but which are not recognised or respected by those of the dominant societies. The idea, for example, that an individual can be delegated to speak for or take decisions for the whole community is against the norms of consensus decision-making which characterise many indigenous peoples' societies. Yet in negotiating with governments, indigenous peoples must elect or select a spokesperson or be disregarded.

Not all indigenous peoples are demanding even separate political rights of a limited kind. What many do want are generally recognised democratic rights. In countries with a proportionately large indigenous population, such as Guatemala, Bolivia, Ecuador and Peru, Indians have been denied any real participation in political affairs since power has been concentrated, by and large, in the hands of the well-off Latinos, people of mixed heritage who regard themselves as Euro–Americans. Where democratic participation has been consistently denied, some indigenous peoples do seek to topple the regimes in power. In these situations, they ally themselves with other organised forces to achieve a common goal.

Whether fighting for political independence or not, all are seeking control over their land and resources. Negotiations between indigenous peoples and governments have generally revolved around issues of size of territory and its inalienability, but also issues of compensation for loss of a share in the wealth extracted, and control over the extent and nature of any outside exploitation of the land. Thus, for example, the new

Nicaraguan constitution guarantees to the indigenous peoples of the eastern region a share in the profits from their resources as well as full authority over their waters and forests, but mineral resources remain under the control of the central government.

Those arguing for a reserve for Brazil's Yanomami Indians maintain that the exclusive use of that land by its indigenous inhabitants is essential for their survival. The reserve needs not only to be demarcated, but strict measures have to be taken to ensure that no settlers or prospectors violate the law. Contact with outsiders has already caused the deaths of many Yanomami from diseases.

In response to Australian Aboriginal demands, the issue of their land rights has been high on the political agenda since the Labour Party victory in 1983. The Labour Party pledged itself to redress the wrong done to Aborigines by providing full land rights in all states and territories of the country. Five key principles emerged from discussions:

* Aboriginal land would be held under inalienable, freehold title.
* Aboriginal sites would be protected.
* Aboriginals would have control in relation to mining on their land.
* Aboriginals would have access to mining royalties or their equivalents.
* Aboriginals would receive compensation for lost land.

The government through its minister for Aboriginal affairs recognised that Aboriginal peoples were the original owners of Australia. Steps were also taken to return sites of religious and cultural importance to their original owners, and in November 1984, Ayers Rock, a massive outcrop in central Australia, was repossessed by the Aboriginal people.

The proposed principles for land rights legislation in Australia contain many of the key demands of indigenous peoples in other countries. They also meet the kinds of objections from vested interests and members of the public which arise elsewhere. 'Yes', the opponents of land rights say, 'let indigenous peoples have a territory, but do not let them stand in the way of national development or prevent the extraction of resources.' On the whole, in Australia, this attitude has prevailed. The Labour Government has back-tracked on the pledge it made in its manifesto on land rights. While it supported action to increase Aboriginal holdings of freehold land, it has refused to implement nationally the controls over mining activities Aboriginal people had requested. The Preferred National Land Rights Model drafted in 1985 by the federal government stated that:

> There is to be no veto over exploration or mining on Aboriginal Land. The formal decision on whether exploration or mining is to proceed on Aboriginal land is to rest with the government.

The proposed model affirms the right to compensation for damage or disturbance to Aboriginal land, but denies Aborigines the right to any share of the wealth generated. Like most indigenous peoples, Aborigines are not claiming privately owned lands, but title to a part of the land owned by the state or already occupied by them. Much of the land claimed by indigenous peoples is unsuitable for intensive agriculture, although it may contain valuable minerals or be suitable for forestry. The indigenous demand is that these activities should take place, if at all, with due respect for religious and cultural sites, with proper compensation for land lost, restoration of land damaged and a just share of the wealth derived from the extraction of natural resources. As owners, indigenous peoples want ultimate control over what takes place on the land. At the present time they are barely consulted.

Indigenous peoples are not, on the whole, asking for anything unreasonable. Many other interest groups, such as environmentalists in certain regions, have more radical demands. Outsiders may even consider the demands of the indigenous to be relatively modest by comparison with the wrongs done to them in the past. It was only with tongue-in-cheek that a Maori teacher, Mgate te Korou, suggested in 1983 that the three million white New Zealanders should be repatriated to their original homelands.[3] Indigenous people accept that their futures are linked to those of the dominant societies which surround them, although they do want an end to domination and repression. In practice, indigenous peoples are not opposed to appropriate economic development if it brings real benefits to their communities. They are not closed to outside influence and values and are ready to adopt practices which may make life less arduous. It is, in fact, certain anthropologists and romanticists who react most strongly to the demise of traditional hand-made clothes or housing constructed of the natural produce of the forest.

Indigenous peoples are not uncompromising in their political and economic demands. They have shown ability in the past to resist their colonisers, retreat with wisdom, and win concessions by negotiation. Their cultures have proven highly resilient, flexible and independent despite concerted efforts to erode them. The survival of indigenous peoples is due to their capacity to borrow what is useful rather than blind commitment to tradition for its own sake.

In essence, indigenous peoples seek recognition, by governments and the international community, of their existence, of their problems and perspectives. They want recognition that their land is essential for their economic, political and spiritual needs and that their methods of production are at no less a stage of development than any other and may even be more ecologically successful than some forms of industrial agriculture. They want recognition of their right to develop their own culture, language and customs. And they seek an end to the victimisation and marginalisation of all indigenous peoples arising from national development, militarisation and ethnocide. The challenge to governments, transnational corporations, and the international community at large is whether they can respond justly to these demands without harming the understandable concerns for general socio-economic and political development.

Governments can begin by abiding by the rule of law, that is by protecting the fundamental human rights of indigenous peoples: the right to life, religious freedom, freedom of expression. Special indigenous demands are now recognised by the international community to be a valid assertion of fundamental human rights, mainly due to indigenous efforts in raising the issue. Those demands revolve around survival, which is integrally tied to the land: Mother Earth.

ISSUES

5.   Mother Earth

Mines

'Whereas it has been known and declared that the poor have no right to the property of the rich, I wish it also to be known and declared that the rich have no right to the property of the poor.'

John Ruskin, 'Unto This Last', 1860

The exploitation of mineral resources, the construction of dams, the building of roads, the opening up of forests by logging companies and cattle ranches – all these activities undertaken in the name of national development have often negatively affected the lives and livelihood of the indigenous people. Contrary to most perceptions, development projects taking place on the marginal lands occupied by them frequently do not bring them higher standards of living and other material benefits. They cause impoverishment and very often long-term degradation of the environment. Of course, this does not need to be so.

If indigenous people were to be consulted by the development planners and given a voice and a role in the implementation of major projects, some real benefits could undoubtedly accrue. But in most cases this is not the practice. Proponents of development claim that the untitled and largely unexploited marginal lands of indigenous peoples are laden with natural wealth. El Dorados are just waiting to be discovered. And improvements in the technology associated with development – exploration by satellites and advanced machinery for mineral extraction – have made it far easier to exploit raw materials in areas which were once totally unexplored and neglected for all practical purposes. In addition, the exhaustion of more readily available raw materials has spurred governments and trans-national corporations to search in new 'frontier' regions. Indigenous people are thus experiencing the consequences of unrelenting competition to discover and lay claim to sources of raw materials.

43

In the last thirty years there has been an increase in the number and intensity of incursions onto land once considered the exclusive territory of indigenous peoples. These lands are considered, by those promoting such development, as unoccupied or as so underpopulated that the fate of the human population should not be seriously considered an obstacle. In 1975 the governor of the state of Roraima in Brazil, answering criticisms of prospecting companies on Yanomami Indian land, stated: 'An area as rich as this, with gold, diamonds and uranium, cannot afford the luxury of preserving half a dozen Indian tribes who are holding back development.'[1] While there may not be many public statements as clear as this, the sentiments behind them are probably common enough.

Like many development projects, mines cause dispossession, sometimes on a large scale. The Greater Carajas project in Brazil's Amazon region will cause the removal of 100,000 people, mostly poor farmers, of whom 10,000 are Indians. In the project area are major deposits of iron ore, bauxite, nickel, manganese and gold. These minerals will be extracted by some of the world's largest mining companies and shipped to a new, specially built port, along a railway link which is being cut expressly for the purpose.[2]

In Panama, a major project to mine an estimated billion tons of copper ore at Cerro Colorado threatens to dispossess the country's largest indigenous population, the Guaymi, of their land. The proposed open-cast mine will cover 330 square kilometres of land and a further 720 square kilometres will be set aside as a concession area for further exploration. Another 630 hectares of land will be needed for the mineworkers' camp and the various access roads. Five Guaymi communities are located in the mining area itself, seven on the site for the construction camp, and three others will be flooded out when a reservoir is built; the road from the port to the mine will pass through 12 other Guaymi villages. An estimated 10,000 Guaymi, one-eighth of their population, will be adversely affected by the project.[3]

Industrialisation on indigenous land acts as a magnet to impoverished and landless outsiders. Although during the construction phase there may be an increase in demand for indigenous workers, this falls off once the industry is set up and skilled and semi-skilled operators are recruited. Industrialisation on indigenous peoples' land, far from being seen as beneficial, is usually rejected by indigenous peoples as being an act of colonisation. In all countries, mining and industrialisation, as they are presently carried out, break down traditional indigenous social organisation. Landless families are forced to migrate into the slums of the new industrial centres and seek work as day labourers; the women may have to enter the job market and undertake work hitherto unknown to them. The breakdown of community and family-based work practices and of the authority of elders has had its impact on the cohesion of indigenous societies. In urban situations, the unemployed indigenous people often resort to alcohol, prostitution and begging to survive in what they perceive as a hostile and alien world.

Mines, perhaps more than other economic development, contribute to the breakdown of the close association of indigenous peoples with their land. Mining transforms familiar landscapes. Mountains and valleys which have been immutable for centuries are turned into featureless wildernesses. Surface 'strip' mining is even more destructive, leaving land unreclaimable. For indigenous peoples, such physical assault on the land itself is seen as desecration. As the Aboriginal organisation, the Federation of Land Councils, has written: 'Because mining threatens the most basic elements in Aboriginal social structure – the land – it confronts directly the integrity of the total fabric of the Aboriginal communities it affects.'[4] Sacred sites have been mined throughout Australia and in one instance an entire sacred mountain in Western Australia was dug up and shipped out in the form of iron ore, without any consultation with its Aboriginal owners.

Adding insult to injury is the fact that the mining projects on indigenous peoples' land, despite the enormous wealth generated, bring little in return to those who are dispossessed and displaced.

The Amungme people lost 10,000 hectares of their traditional lands to the Freeport copper mine in West Papua (the Indonesian province of Irian Jaya), and only received minimal compensation. The mine – 85 per cent foreign owned – had gross sales exceeding US\$ 150 million in 1980. As a tribal elder commented: 'It is like having a coconut tree growing in your garden. The coconuts grow but fall in places far from home. The only things that fall in our garden are the leaves and other rubbish which despoil our land.'[5]

The Guaymi have argued that the Cerro Colorado mine on their land will benefit the non-indigenous Panamanians and not the Indian people. They fear that the influx of outsiders will introduce prostitution, gambling and crime. If the experience of similar projects in the Amazon area and North America is anything to go by, then they may be right. Thousands of non-indigenous male workers earning comparatively good wages attract entrepreneurs ready to sell alcohol, sex and gambling. Meanwhile, as the Guaymi are displaced, they join the ranks of poorly paid migrant workers in places like the United Fruit plantations in Costa Rica.

Similar fears about the social disintegration of indigenous communities caused by mining were expressed in an Australian government report in 1977. The Fox Report, which examined the impact of the Ranger Uranium Mine on Aboriginal people in the Northern Territory, stated: 'The arrival of large numbers of white people in the region will potentially be very damaging to the welfare and interests of the Aboriginal people there.' The report went on to express concern about Aboriginal unemployment, health (particularly venereal disease and alcoholism), racial tensions and conflicts, the likely deterioration in morale and the overwhelming opposition of Aboriginal people. However, the report concluded that, despite these misgivings, the 'national interest' should prevail.

Yet where mining has taken place on Aboriginal lands, these apprehensions have proved well founded. The relationships between white employers with money and high social status and the largely poor and unemployed Aboriginal population are sources of permanent conflict. On the tensions between the two communities one Aboriginal woman, Marcia Langton, has commented:

'They cause jealousy, tension and often violence between Aboriginal and White man; they disrupt the complex and important kinship patterns in Aboriginal society and they produce children who are neither a part of the traditional scheme, nor are they wanted or accepted as part of white society, yet it is the

Aboriginal community which takes them and works them in and looks after them. Most alarmingly, these encounters have introduced venereal diseases. Only ten years ago, syphilis was virtually unknown in this region; it is now almost plague proportions and getting worse.'[6]

National interest is invariably invoked by the government when it is seeking to promote mining and other kinds of industrialisation on land occupied by indigenous peoples. However, critics of the Carajas Project in Brazil, who include scientists and economists, point out that one-third of the total investment of US$ 30 billion comes from abroad.[7] These foreign investors have been attracted to the project by massive government subsidies for the necessary infrastructure – rail links, roads, electricity, ports and housing – and by tax concessions and the lifting of exchange controls. For the remaining investment, Brazil – one of the world's most indebted nations – has raised loans on the international market. That there are profits for the foreign investors and national companies engaged in the projects there is little doubt, but that indigenous people or even other ordinary Brazilians benefit is less certain.

In poor countries, mining exerts a powerful influence over governments and wins highly advantageous conditions for its investments. Nations facing large deficits in balance of payments may be tempted to accept unfavourable terms in order to attract foreign companies. In the case of the Cerro Colorado project in Panama, for example, the state-owned company, although the majority shareholder, held fewer voting rights than the foreign company, Rio Tinto Zinc, partnering the venture. Panamanian personnel had limited experience of large mining operations, lacked technical and financial expertise and were, therefore, susceptible to the directives of the foreign investor. The World Bank, approached by Panama for a loan to cover the major part of its share of the equity, estimated that the government could expect a zero or negative income for the first six years of operations, while its foreign partner would receive, under the terms of the agreement, an income of over US$ 170 million, thereby recouping nearly all of its initial investment. In addition, the government of Panama was expected to cover all infrastructural expenses, which would include improved port

47

facilities, roads and a greatly enhanced hydro-electric capacity.[8]

Even in rich countries, mining generates enormous personal wealth for investors. Companies that would never consider suggesting a mining operation in the middle of a large city, causing relocation of people, have no compunction about invading the Navajo and Cheyenne Indian reservations in the Western parts of the US. An estimated 20,000 Navajos, ten per cent of their total population, are being relocated in Arizona, to make way for coal strip mining.

Severe and permanent environmental damage may also be done by mining. In American Indian and Aboriginal reserves mining can leave land virtually unreclaimable. The resulting pollution may also seriously affect the health of the indigenous inhabitants. In the USA, for example, uranium mining is responsible for an increase in the number of deaths of native people. Between 1971 and 1980, 25 of the 700 Navajos working on the Kerr-McGee uranium mines and mills on the Navajo reservation died of lung cancer. This is a rate of cancer death 400 per cent higher than the national average.[9] According to a statement by the International Indian Treaty Council in 1981, 'More and more Indian populations which live near uranium mining areas are found to have elevated birth defect rates, higher leukemia levels, and a greater number of cancers of the lung, skin, bladder and digestive tract. This is attributable to the contamination of the environment.'[10]

In Australia, uranium has been discovered in huge quantities on Aboriginal reserves, and is now being mined. The Australian Council of Churches in a report in 1977 warned that the pollution of food supplies would cause long-term illness among the Aborigines.[11] Mining companies, however, are concerned with profit and do their best to reduce expenditure whether on compensation to the Aboriginal owners of the land or on subsequent reclamation. They often have important political allies in the government and can also dispose of substantial funds for public relations. The London paper, the *Financial Times*, on 23 June 1981 reported that a subsidiary of the mining company Rio Tinto Zinc had hired Australia's largest public relations firm 'to hold down the proportion of the wealth generated by the mine that would be returned as payments in royalties to the Aboriginals.'

Lawful mining is not the only problem; the numerous illegal or semi-legal operations undertaken by outside prospectors also represent a threat to indigenous peoples. Since 1983 Amazonia has experienced a flood of mainly poor miners into the area. At the frontier of Brazil and Venezuela, the heartland of Yanomami territory has been invaded by hundreds of miners. These uncontrolled incursions have led to conflicts between miners and Indians and caused several deaths. The Union of Indian Nations, the main organisation of Brazilian Indians, stated in 1985 that illegal mining was affecting four main Indian areas.[12] Brazilian and foreign mining companies have applied for mining permits in 43 per cent of Indian territory in the state of Para and the territory of Amapa.[13]

At the heart of the problem is the right of indigenous peoples to the land they occupy. Even where the governments have guaranteed reserves to indigenous peoples, these have generally not included rights to the natural resources of the land. In some countries – Australia, for example – there may be a limited protection of sites of religious or cultural importance; and in the USA, Australia and Canada various agreements about royalty payments and compensation have been made. But governments retain the final say over whether indigenous peoples' land will be mined and the conditions which will apply.

Indigenous peoples are now demanding greater control over the economic development occurring on their land. The Guaymi of Panama have successfully blocked the Cerro Colorado project and are negotiating with the government for their own territory and recognition of a Guaymi Congress as the highest decision-making body. The Aboriginal peoples of Australia have generated widespread support from liberal white opinion, the church and trade unions, for their opposition to mining on their land. In its July 1984 conference the Labour Party of Australia resolved to introduce legislation which would give Aboriginal people 'the right to refuse permission for mining on their land and to impose conditions under which mining may proceed' (a pledge the government of Australia has not yet redeemed). Support from the international indigenous lobby played a role in these reversals.

Although indigenous peoples are, in general, opposed to mining on their land, there are cases in the United States or

49

Australia where mutually acceptable arrangements have been made. The Pitjantjatjara people of Australia, for example, have negotiated with mining companies and set up their own prospecting enterprises. But such examples are rare and their outcome uncertain. Most mining on indigenous peoples' land causes confrontation and conflict. It brings together, head on, two opposing world views – one based on nationally planned, large-scale mechanised industrial development, and the other centred on a small-scale, labour-intensive, low energy-consuming, self-reliant and environmentally protective way of life. Indigenous peoples have a non-exploitative relationship with the land based on subsistence needs, while Western society sees nature as an object to be harnessed for its own material advancement and the production of surplus wealth. Of course, such a dichotomy oversimplifies a range of attitudes towards nature among indigenous and non-indigenous people, but if indigenous peoples are to be protected from rapacious mining operations, schemes which accord greater respect to their right to land and natural resources must be devised.

The future of mining itself, as well as petroleum extraction, is unclear. These are non-renewable resources. Governments are not pressuring energy corporations to carry out more research on renewable energy resources, nor are governments investing in such research adequately. The vocal demands of indigenous peoples in this respect will prove beneficial to humankind. Meanwhile, all indigenous land should be made inalienable and secure, mining operations should be re-examined and, if necessary, suspended when the indigenous community is seriously affected and so demands.

Dams

'It is a bad plan that admits of no modification.'

Publilius Syrus, 1st century B.C.

They had their first inkling about the dam when the construction of the workers' quarters began. There were no visits by officials to inform the indigenous inhabitants, just the

50

arrival one day of a bulldozer, a lorry-load of building materials and a dozen workers from outside the state. The indigenous people, curious to know what was afoot, chatted with the workers but could not be sure. A dam, they thought. The people looked at their river, their valley, and the green patches of forest on the slopes. They had heard about dams before. They knew their reservoirs submerged entire villages and forests. There had been news of dams in other parts of the country displacing thousands of people and leaving them landless and penniless. They were impatient to find out more.

This was 1979. As their village swelled with workers and engineers, the local inhabitants had their worst fears confirmed. The hydro-electric project would dam their river and the reservoir would submerge 17 villages and affect 13 others. About 7,000 people would have to leave their homes and land, and a further 4,000 to 5,000 others would lose some or all of their land. Some 2,700 acres of agricultural land would be flooded. The more than 10,000 inhabitants, 95 per cent of whom were indigenous people, were due to face an unparalleled social upheaval.

By the time they learnt about the project, the planning of the dam had already reached a point of no return. They were offered labouring jobs, but refused them. The construction company imported more workers from outside the state. Slowly the colossal structure took shape. The indigenous people, resigned to the inevitable, began to seek compensation for the loss of their homes, land and livelihood. But they were soon disappointed. Of the 2,700 acres of agricultural land due to be flooded, they learned, 1,600 acres were unregistered and the occupants were, therefore, not entitled to compensation. Compensation for the remaining 1,100 acres was considered well below its real value and even then not paid in time. Income-producing trees were either not compensated for or the compensation was derisory. Of the 676 households entitled to resettlement, 315 had been allocated 0.25 acres of homestead land, sufficient for a house and a garden, in a nearby village. But the land made available for resettlement was already occupied by the villagers, a large proportion of whom were themselves landless or land poor.[14]

This real life story from a South Asian country illustrates

what has happened to scores of indigenous communities in practically all parts of the world. Dams, like mines, cause incalculable harm to indigenous societies. But the reasons why governments build dams are unequivocal. Dams provide the energy to fuel industrialisation and stimulate employment and development. 'After the dam, our land will be paradise,' chanted the Egyptian people while the Aswan dam was being built. The reservoirs store water for massive irrigation schemes which bring improvements in agricultural production. Dams provide jobs. The original Mahaweli dam project in Sri Lanka, for example, was expected to create nearly half a million agricultural and related jobs.[15] Results have not only been short of expectations but have brought many unexpected ills, environmental and social, in their wake.

Hydro-electric power is cheap as compared to energy generation from a thermal plant; it also reduces dependence on fossil fuel imports. Cheap energy and a store of irrigation water are alluring prospects for governments and, consequently, dams have become the core components of their development strategies.

Dam construction has escalated since the 1960s and each new project appears more massive than the last. By 1990 there are expected to be 113 superdams – dams over 150 metres high – in the world. Most of them will be in Africa, Asia and Latin America. The World Bank – one of the major funders of these projects – estimates that US$ 100 billion will be spent on these projects over the next two decades. However, there is now serious criticism of large dams. Hydro-electric projects, the critics say, cause the loss of agricultural land and forests. They also displace huge numbers of people – for example, 78,000 were evacuated to make way for the Volta dam in Ghana and 450,000 were displaced by the Pa Mong project in Vietnam. The large artificial lakes are breeding grounds for water-borne diseases, particularly malaria and schistosomiasis. Nor are the dams achieving the objectives laid out by their planners. Siltation rates of the reservoirs of some major dams are several times greater than anticipated. The life-span of the Tehri dam in India may be just 30 or 40 years instead of the proposed 100 years, and the Pelegre dam in Haiti, built to last 50 years, is about to be decommissioned after only 30 years.[16] In India no irrigation or hydro-electric project since 1951 has been completed on time or within the cost estimate. Indeed, according to the Irrigation Minister, R. N. Mirdha, in 1983, 32 major projects showed cost overruns of 500 per cent or more.[17]

Superdams are extremely costly: the Mahaweli dam in Sri Lanka is expected to cost US$ 1.2 billion; the final costs of the Narmada River Basin Development project in India are estimated at over US$ 20 billion; in the Philippines the hydro-electric power generating programme for the ten years 1979 to 1988 was calculated at US$ 6.4 billion.[18] Since most of the funding comes in the form of foreign loans from multilateral development banks, such projects represent a long-term commitment of reserves and a diversion of a major part of national revenue from development alternatives.

The lands of indigenous peoples are vulnerable to dam-building programmes. As already pointed out, these peoples are politically weaker than other groups and often occupy so-called public land and, therefore, have no titles to ownership. The prevailing view among many government officials is that the benefits of hydro-electric power far outweigh the political and economic costs involved in displacing indigenous populations in the project area. This is true to the extent that the land occupied by indigenous peoples is less populated than in other rural areas. Indeed many of these territories do not naturally support large populations. Nevertheless, they do support indigenous peoples and may have done so for thousands of years. The inundation of a fertile valley bottom and forested slopes which may be used for shifting cultivation and hunting and gathering, can therefore destroy the life support system of indigenous peoples.

The dislocations and the areas of land submerged by hydro-electric projects often occur on a huge scale. The Karnaphuli reservoir in the Chittagong Hill Tracts of Bangladesh submerged 250 square miles of prime agricultural land, making up 40 per cent of the cultivable area of the region. About 100,000 indigenous people – one-sixth of the total population – were displaced.[19] The Chico River Basin development programme in the Philippines – postponed after local resistance – would have destroyed 16 villages, flooded nearly 3,000 hectares of rice terraces and uprooted 90,000 people. Ironically, the rice yields from the terraces are as much as three times the national average and the standard family holding of half a hectare is able to satisfy basic needs. The overall energy development programme in the Philippines, which will affect the major rivers of the country, threatens the mountain homes of many different indigenous peoples and a total of 1.5 million people.[20]

In the west of India, one of the most ambitious development schemes in the world is planned along the Narmada River. The series of major dams will cause the submergence of 375,000 hectares of land and displace hundreds of thousands of people. One dam alone – the Sardar Sarovar – will reportedly inundate 235 villages, flood 40,000 hectares of agricultural land and force from their homes 120,000 people – of whom a sizeable proportion are indigenous.[21]

Dams also threaten indigenous peoples in Latin America. There are seven hydro-electric projects either planned or in progress on indigenous peoples' land in Brazil. More than 30 Indian areas will be affected and at least 100,000 hectares of indigenous homelands will be flooded or otherwise expropriated for the projects.[22] The Tucurui dam in the north-eastern state of Para has inundated 2,000 square kilometres of forest, part of which comprised territory officially recognised by the government as the homeland of the Parakanas.[23] In Guyana a proposed hydro-electric scheme in the Upper Mazaruni district will flood 1,000 square miles of land and displace 5,000 Akawaio Indians.[24]

As in the case of mines, the indigenous peoples affected by dam-building are rarely consulted or adequately compensated. The people uprooted by the Karnaphuli reservoir in the Chittagong Hill Tracts of Bangladesh owned on average six acres of good rice land before the dam was constructed. But in compensation they were offered only three acres of land of comparable quality. Most of the rest of the community did not receive any land or financial compensation.[25] Of course, the truth is that there is very often no other good land available for compensation once the valley bottoms are submerged and those displaced are forced to move onto hill slopes already occupied by other farmers. The demand often made by indigenous peoples of 'land for land' cannot be satisfied in many cases. Obviously, it is during the planning process of a project that the interests of the populations which would be affected, and all other relevant humanitarian considerations, should be taken fully into account.

Even when financial compensation is made, it hardly replaces the relatively secure livelihood offered by land. Cash is rapidly spent on the daily necessities of life no longer supplied by the land, or else spent on consumer goods brought in by outside tráders. Of those families which had received compensation following the construction of the Kutku dam in India, for example, more than three-quarters had spent their entire funds within six months.[26] These unfortunate families, unused to a cash economy, are easily exploited by unscrupulous traders, and are then left destitute. The cash compensation to those displaced by the Koel Karo dam in Bihar, India, was disbursed in such small instalments and through so long a process of applications, that in some cases only between five and ten per cent of the award was actually received. The rest was reportedly pocketed by agents, lawyers and petty officials.[27]

Very few government rehabilitation schemes provide free advice to displaced peoples about how to use their compensation constructively; nor do they provide for any vocational training or employment component. Agriculturalists with no other knowledge but farming have no alternative than to migrate to the towns in search of work as unskilled labourers. Consideration of the future job prospects of the indigenous peoples dispossessed of their lands is invariably absent, or else given low priority, in the project specifications. The World Bank, which has adopted special policy guidelines in order to protect indigenous peoples, allocates only a tiny part of any project's budget to the costs of rehabilitation. In the case of the Sardar Sarovar dam in the state of Madhya Pradesh, India, only one per cent of the US$ 300 million being lent by the Bank has been set aside for relocation costs. Indeed, more is being spent on building the temporary colony for the 5,000 employees of the dam than for the more than 100,000 people due to lose their homes and land.[28]

Dams, however, have more than an economic impact on indigenous peoples. The flooding of their land may also be an assault on their history and culture. The Kalinga and Bontoc peoples of the Philippines consider their valleys to be the spiritual homes of their ancestors whom they honour and respect. The Narmada river – like many in India – is sacred to the peoples dependent on it. The dams built across the Fort George river in north-west Quebec disturbed the traditional territories of the Cree and other native peoples, not only threatening their livelihoods but their identity as a people. Phillip Awashish, a Cree spokesman, has noted that: 'the way of life created in the bush – hunting, fishing, trapping – is a spiritual way of life . . . and therefore constitutes part of the religion of the Cree Nation.'[29]

The Sami people (Lapps) have made similar objections to the hydro-electric project on the Alta river in Norway. Although the number of Sami immediately affected is small, the location of the dam in the heartland of an open tundra supporting 60,000 reindeer, is likely to have far-reaching socio-economic consequences for them.[30] The hydro-electric project will disturb established patterns of reindeer pastoralism and further weaken the Sami people's relationship with the land. The threat to the Sami is economic for the ten per cent that practise reindeer herding, but also symbolic for all Sami: the construction of the dam is an invasion of their land and a testimony to their powerlessness in the face of the dominant society.

Most indigenous peoples do not benefit in any way from the massive investments required for dam construction. In many cases they are not even employed as labourers since employers prefer to bring in contract workers from outside the area. Even where displaced indigenous peoples are used in the construction, they are not retained as part of the permanent maintenance staff for the dam. The electricity produced by the project is not generally available to the indigenous population or the local rural poor. In the Philippines, for example, the majority of rural inhabitants live on incomes so low that they could never afford the electric connection and yearly standing charges. Most indigenous villages remain without electricity, while high above their homes and fields cables stretch from pylon to pylon, from the power station to the towns and their factories. The biggest customers for the 8,000 megawatts of electricity produced by the Tucurui dam in Brazil are the railway, the nearby Carajas iron ore project and an aluminium smelter 600 kilometres away in Belem.[31] The Indian communities uprooted by all this electrification and industrialisation remain with their kerosene lamps. Few Navajos have electricity even in Arizona, USA, though the gigantic hydro-electric project on their land fuels the lights of Las Vegas and Los Angeles.

It should not be imagined, however, that indigenous peoples passively look on as their forests and fields are flooded. Often they have no knowledge of the hydro-electric projects until construction begins, but once aware of the plans indigenous peoples have acted rapidly to register their protest. When the James Bay hydro-electric project in Quebec, Canada, was announced, native peoples – on whose land it was due to be built – took their case to court and won an injunction to stop construction. They entered into direct negotiations with the government of Quebec and achieved numerous modifications to the original proposal. But such legal expedients are not always possible. For years the indigenous people who will be displaced by the Koel Karo dam in India have delayed construction by acts of civil disobedience and now face threats of forcible removal.

The Chico River Basin development project in the Philippines met determined and organised resistance from the mainly Kalinga and Bontoc communities whose homes were threatened by flooding. They called mass meetings, held demonstrations and petitioned former President Marcos and the World Bank, which was providing much of the funding. The government brought in troops to put down the opposition, but repression only pushed the people into joining the New People's Army, the armed wing of the Philippines Communist Party, which was active in the area. Unable to ensure the safety of construction teams, the World Bank withdrew its support for the project. The lesson that only armed resistance produces results is not lost on powerless indigenous peoples.

Increasingly, dams affecting indigenous peoples are being recognised as damaging to the wider environment and therefore attracting criticism. Since the government of Malaysia declared its intention to build the Bakun dam in Sarawak, environmental groups in the country have thrown themselves into whole-hearted opposition. They maintain that the US$ 2 billion

57

hydro-electric project will increase the foreign debt by 20 per cent, inundate 600 square kilometres of rain forest and displace at least 10,000 indigenous people. They also question the technical feasibility of the 650 kilometre submarine high-voltage cable from Sarawak to the main electricity load centres on peninsular Malaysia.[32]

Large dams are disastrous for indigenous peoples. They destroy their economies and habitats, disrupt their social systems, and submerge and otherwise desecrate sites of religious or cultural importance. Indigenous communities are dispersed, losing their original cohesion and unity; they are left impoverished, often landless and dispirited. As Ellen Johnsen Turi, a Sami herder, told an investigating team from the Supreme Court of Norway: 'The authorities are destroying our occupations so that other and better people can have work and be paid good wages. I would not call that democracy. It is the politics of annihilation.'[33] Even without consideration of the social, environmental and human costs, giant dams are rarely cost effective. A US Department of Energy study in 1977 argued convincingly that six small dams which do not cause flooding or destruction of water life, are more cost-effective than one large dam. However, the profits from construction are much less. Gigantic industrial contractors exert powerful political influence on governments and lending institutions.

In the context of the welfare of the indigenous people and indeed the population as a whole, the point is not so much to halt hydro-electric projects or stop the construction of dams, but rather to have a more holistic approach to such development projects, as well as to develop alternative energy sources. National policies should take into account more fully the welfare of people directly affected, and particularly, the most vulnerable among them: the indigenous populations.

Forests

'Trees are the earth's endless effort to speak to the listening heavens.'
Rabindranath Tagore, 1920

Until 1974 the Karen villagers hardly saw an outsider. Their village in the Mae Hong Son district of North-west Thailand

58

was a four hour walk from the nearest road, mostly uphill and through thick forest. In the summer the journey was exhausting, the heat and humidity were debilitating and the slopes seemingly unending. In the rainy season the trek – lengthened by the slippery state of the narrow path and the regular stops to pick off the leeches – could take an extra hour or two. When the agents from the logging company arrived waving pieces of paper and talking about concessions, they attracted the curiosity of the local people. But their welcome was short-lived. They explained that they had government permission to fell trees in the area. The elders unanimously objected.

A month later the agents returned. They told the people that only the big trees would be cut and that the company would be building an access road which would make travel to and from the village easier. They also said that there would be work available for the villagers and that a percentage of the trees cut would be given to their community. Some of the elders signed the agreement. For those who dissented, the agents had brought another piece of paper. This, it was explained, would be presented to the forest department to show there was opposition. But as it turned out, the document was an agreement giving the logging company permission to fell their trees. Since most of the villagers were Karen-speakers who could not read Thai, they had taken the agents' word for the contents of the document.

The access road was built and the company began its operations. The villagers complained to the district administration but no notice was taken. The logging company, having felled the large trees, began cutting down all the timber in the concession area. The community collected money to pay for one of the better educated Karen to go to the district administration once more and plead their case. On his return he was shot and wounded by a hired gunman. He told his story to the police but was accused of being a trouble-maker and a communist sympathiser and threatened with imprisonment. The shooting and the threat of police violence stopped their protests.

A little over a decade later, the village can now be reached easily by road. The company concession has expanded and entirely surrounds the village. Not a single indigenous villager was employed by the company and none received any compensation, even though they lost their gardens and all the fruit trees they had planted. Before the company arrived, the surrounding forest was used for shifting cultivation and the community was more or less self-sufficient in rice and other basic foods, such as fruit and vegetables. Today, they have to walk ten kilometres to reach their fields, a journey which takes two and a half hours each way. The new land is considerably less fertile than the old area. Of the 100 or so households in the village, only ten now have a rice surplus and more than one-third do not have enough to eat. Many have had no choice but to work as low-paid labourers for local Thai farmers.

Now the very survival of the community is in question. Before the company came, the trees on either side of the nearby river had been preserved so as not to interfere with its course; these have now been felled and the water supply seriously affected. Even the government's fitful reforestation programme is further reducing the economic viability of the community by forbidding animal grazing in replanted areas. In another decade this tiny community, like hundreds of others in this forested region of Thailand, will have dispersed.[34]

There are perhaps some 200 million people living in and around the world's forests, but the great majority are non-indigenous migrants who have moved there in the last two or three decades.[35] The indigenous inhabitants, those whose ancestors have lived in the forests for thousands of years and learned how to live in harmony with the complex environment, are far fewer. But figures are hard to estimate.

Tropical forests cover more than 3.6 million square miles, in West and Central Africa, Central America and Amazonia and in parts of South and South East Asia. Many of them have long been the home of indigenous peoples. Slash-and-burn agriculturists have lived in the Ituri forest in Zaire, for example, for 2,000 years.

The indigenous inhabitants of the forests living in their traditional way are able to supply all their subsistence needs from their surroundings. There are of course enormous variations in the form of agro–forestry they adopt, but essentially they are entirely self-sufficient or else have some long-standing exchange relationship with neighbouring communities. The predominant mode of agricultural production is shifting cultivation. An area of forest is cleared, planted for one season, and then left fallow for several years. Some, like the Miskito and Sumu Indians of Eastern Nicaragua and Honduras, keep their village in one place and rotate their fields in the surrounding cleared areas. Shifting cultivation is capable of sustaining many more people than hunting and gathering and, provided there is sufficient land, is an ecologically sound method of farming forested areas. Some indigenous peoples also farm the valley bottoms on a fixed field system or – as in the Philippines – build terraces for crops such as rice. In Zaire, the Mbuti (Pygmies) hunt game and gather honey which they exchange for vegetables and other cultivated foods grown by Bantu farmers. In the Brazilian Amazon and eastern parts of Central America, Indians often combine semi-nomadic hunting, fishing and gathering with permanent gardens where they plant subsistence crops and vegetables.

The various kinds of agro–forestry practised by indigenous peoples were and, to a large extent still are, regarded by many development planners as inefficient and unproductive. But this is far from true. Forest dwellers possess a deep knowledge of their environment which scientists are only now beginning to recognise. The Lawa people of Northern Thailand, for example, grow 75 food crops, 21 medicinal plants and numerous others for ceremonial and decorative use.[36] In Garhsaru, a tribal village in Bihar, India, one local person was able to point out in the course of a walk of just one hundred metres, trees and plants which produced fruit, fibre for rope, oil for wounds and snakebites, fruit for chutney and cold sherbets, leaves which could be boiled to cure headaches and stomach complaints, leaves which could be dried for use as an anti-diarrhoeal, leaves suitable as vegetables or for making alcohol, twigs for toothbrushes, and seeds whose oil could produce an ointment for eye infections. There were also bamboos which were tender to eat, whose leaves served as forage for the animals, and when dried could be turned into baskets; there were trees which were suitable for the cultivation of lac – the raw material from which furniture polish is made – and trees which produced only fuelwood. However, where the products of the forests have been commercialised, as happened during the rubber boom, indigenous communities may become cash dependent, and over-exploit the resources for the market. This was true of the Miskitos of Nicaragua in the 1920s.

The knowledge passed on from generation to generation allows indigenous people to exploit the forest without doing it any long-term harm provided they are self-subsistent. The forest agricultural practices of mixed cropping, no tillage – the earth is not turned and seeds are planted in small holes made with a dibble – and long fallow periods ensure that the thin tropical soils are not overused. It is a system which is not only environmentally sound but also often more productive than high technology alternatives.

Many indigenous peoples also derive their only income from gathering or processing minor forest produce. In India, sales of these products account for as much as 30 per cent of the earnings of people in some areas of the country.[37] But very often the relationship between indigenous peoples and the forest goes beyond mere material inter-dependence. Mbuti (Pygmies) think of the forest as their father and mother providing 'food, clothing, shelter, warmth and affection.'[38] In many forest-dwelling communities there are sacred areas. In India, for example, sacred groves or *sarnas* are never farmed or felled. Sometimes certain species of trees are also regarded as sacred. These special parts of the forest are symbols of the harmonious relationship between forest and forest dweller.

However, the close association of forest dwellers with their environment is being rapidly eroded. The very forest itself is disappearing from our planet. Since 1950, according to the United Nations Food and Agricultural Organisation, over half of the world's forests have been destroyed. Some estimates put the destruction or degradation of tropical forest at 50 million acres annually. That is about 100 acres per minute. And the pressures on the forests are increasing. In 1970 a small team in Amazonia could clear 2.5 acres of forest a day, now two bulldozers with a chain between them rip out 100 acres daily. Already there are fears that at the present rate, Thailand, Malaysia, the Philippines, Guatemala and Panama will have no significant areas of forest left by the end of the century. The greatest rain forest in the world – the Amazon – is expected to lose nearly 100,000 square miles of forest, an area larger than the United Kingdom, by the year 2000.[39] There is general agreement that such relentless deforestation not only threatens irreversible climatic changes but also an irreparable loss of the gene pools we require for future agricultural and medical progress.

The causes of deforestation are ungoverned short-term development as well as desperation. Development because governments have seen their forests as sources of immense natural wealth; and desperation because many landless peasants have moved into these environments to escape the wretched poverty of their own regions. Together these two pressures are destroying countless indigenous communities and the forest on which they depend.

Invasions of the forest by outsiders are nothing new. At the turn of the century large areas of the Upper Amazon were inundated by rubber tappers and speculators. At about the same time, the banana companies began establishing plantations and cutting wood in Central America. In 19th century India, the British colonial authorities turned vast regions of forests into reserves, thereby restricting the movement of the indigenous inhabitants. But the scale of the present invasion is unprecedented. The commercial exploitation of timber and cattle ranching and other kinds of agribusiness have caused as much dislocation and human suffering as development projects for mineral extraction or for the production of hydro-electric power.

The demand for hardwoods, mostly to be found in tropical forests, has increased markedly in the last 30 years. The main markets are the Western industrialised nations and Japan. As noted earlier, the appetites of these countries for wood of this type has jumped from four million cubic metres in 1950 to 70 million in 1985; by the year 2000 that figure may well exceed 100 million. The major producers of hardwood – the Philippines, Malaysia and Indonesia – now earn an important part of their foreign exchange from timber. In 1980, for example, Indonesia's foreign revenue from timber was greater than from all its other agricultural commodities together.[40] In the world's forests themselves, industrial logging accounts for about 20 per cent of the total area lost each year.[41]

Commercial felling is generally more harmful to the native inhabitants and the environment than is immediately obvious. Large profits can be made from logging. In the Mae Hong Son district of Northern Thailand a good-sized teak tree can fetch over US$ 850, but the government tax is only one per cent. In the 11 concession areas marked out by the forestry department, there are 30 lots each containing an average of 2,500 teaks and a further 5,000 other saleable trees. The seven companies which won the concessions from the government are all owned by the same person, a retired army general and former member of parliament.[42] Even with legal felling, the profits are colossal. The total value of teak exports alone are over US$ 700 million. But the companies are taking out all the trees, even immature ones whose felling is not allowed by the forest department; they are straying outside the concession areas and bulldozing the stumps to destroy any evidence. The concession areas extend along both sides of a river near which dozens of Karen communities are settled. These people gain nothing from the timber exploitation – neither employment nor compensation – and can only watch helplessly as their source of livelihood disappears forever. Similarly, the Mayans in Mexico find their mahogany forests disappearing to make way for cattle ranching.

As a consequence of widespread commercial logging, governments have taken some mitigating action by setting up reforestation programmes. These schemes have been substantially supported during the last few years by foreign donors and loans from the World Bank and other multilateral development banks. The policies of reforestation have been particularly favoured by the government of India. India's social forestry scheme, so called to denote the fact that its target is the rural poor, is proving controversial. A former member of the Planning Commission's Working Group on Energy Policies has commented: 'I have seen many programmes launched in the name of the poor but soon distorted to benefit the upper classes. But no programme has been diverted further away from its objective than social forestry.'[43]

In general, the positive impact of social forestry on the indigenous communities living in the forests has been negligible. They complain that the forest department plants mainly fast-growing commercial trees, such as eucalyptus, which provide no fodder for the animals. Such monocultural plantations contain none of the variety of foods, medicines, and other necessities which the original mixed forests held in abundance. The replanted forests are also subject to much stricter controls by forest department officials, who are at liberty to deny their use to the local people. As they lose control over what previously was their familiar environment, indigenous people become less involved in its conservation. Forest officials have also been susceptible to bribery from commercial loggers seeking to take trees out of the reserve. There has been a deterioration of the forests since control passed to the forest department rather than the local community. The problem with reforestation, as with deforestation, is that the trees – whether they are being planted or being cut down – remain big business.

In Latin America cattle ranching and other agribusiness activities are probably the single largest cause of deforestation. It has been estimated that in the region of 20,000 square kilometres of forest fall victim to cattle ranchers each year. In Costa Rica, for example, pasture has more than doubled since 1950. Most of the new land claimed from the forest is now worked out and abandoned. The production of beef is three and a half times greater than it was in 1961. Yet two-thirds of the cattle are exported and the *per capita* consumption of meat in the country has declined by nearly half since 1960. In Brazil over 100,000 square kilometres of forest lands were converted to cattle ranches.[44] Some of the ranches, owned by corporations or rich Sao Paulo families, covered areas of more than 2,000 square kilometres. Those buying these vast pieces of territory could have no idea of the number of indigenous people living there. Conflicts between Indians and ranchers became inevitable. Nine Indian villages were located on over 3.5 million acres of forest bought by a United States shipping millionnaire for timber extraction and cattle rearing. The cattle ranch owned by Volkswagen of Brazil in the State of Para occupies part of Indian traditional land. When speculation in land is on such a vast scale, it is perhaps inevitable that the indigenous inhabitants are ignored or deemed obstacles to economic gain.

'Development' has not been alone in bringing about the alienation of indigenous peoples' land and destruction of the forests. Population growth and land hunger have exerted a pressure on forest dwellers and their environment. The massive programmes of relocation of populations sponsored by governments to accommodate poor landless peasants have been a major cause of deforestation and conflict. The great influx of outsiders into the tropical forests – into, for example, the Amazonian regions of Peru, Ecuador and Brazil; the Mosquitia of Honduras and Nicaragua or Chiapas in Mexico; the provinces of Irian Jaya and Kalimantan in Indonesia, or the hill tracts of South-east Bangladesh – have disrupted traditional indigenous agricultural methods, such as shifting cultivation. In many of these places, indigenous communities have been forced onto much smaller areas of land and have consequently had to shorten drastically the fallow periods of their fields. Instead of allowing them time to regenerate, indigenous farmers are being driven to clear and plant the same plot every two or three years. This enforced practice is causing permanent damage to the ecosystem and threatens to undermine the economic system of millions of indigenous people.

Indigenous peoples are well aware of the destruction to the forest ecology this practice causes, but there is little alternative left to them. Pushed off their traditional lands, they are no longer able to feed themselves from forest produce. Instead they are forced to earn an income in whatever way they can. In many places, the only source of income is from the collection of fuelwood. The women – since they are mainly responsible for the collection of fuelwood – must travel further and further afield in search of wood as the forest is depleted. They are aware of the environmental dangers to the forest. But, deprived of the means to survive by exploiting the forest without destroying it, and with no other employment opportunities, they struggle for a living in the only way available.

The impact on the indigenous peoples of forest lands by outsiders has been far-reaching. In the last 30 years traditional agro–forestry practices have been seriously affected. The balanced relationship of indigenous people with the forest has been eroded and many have been forced to move from their territories. It would be a mistake to believe that this has happened without protest and resistance. Indigenous peoples have fought back. Numerous incoming settlers have been attacked and killed by Brazilian Indians and in India the pacific Chipko movement, where women came out and hugged the trees to save them, became an example throughout the region. But, on the whole, forest dwellers are isolated and politically weak. They often know nothing of the developments being planned by government officials and outside consultants until too late. In any case, since most have no legal title to the land they live on, they face the combined force of the settlers, the courts, the police and in extreme cases the army. The greatest hope now for many indigenous peoples is that governments and development planners are slowly beginning to acknowledge that their understanding of the tropical forest environment is actually limited, and that the grandiose schemes devised in the world's capitals are not always in the national interest and indeed may well be harmful to the future development of the country.

Some examples which offer hope for forests and forest dwellers, and which other countries should emulate, are: the recognition by the government of India in its latest five-year plan that indigenous communities should be involved in the management of the forests; the decision by the government of Panama to support the Kuna Indians of San Blas in their forest conservation activities; the provisions in the 1987 Nicaraguan constitution which guarantee full local control of forests within the autonomy plan for the indigenous people living in the eastern region of the country.

6. Struggle for Survival

Relocations

'It is natural anywhere that people like their own kind, but it is not necessarily natural that their fondness for their own kind should lead them to the subjection of whole groups of other people not like them.'

Pearl S. Buck, 1943

Mines, dams and commercial logging bring outsiders into indigenous peoples' territories, but in comparatively small numbers. Government-sponsored programmes of relocation of populations, however, are radically altering the demographic balance of regions of low population density where indigenous peoples live. Economic development projects cause the alienation of a part of the territory of indigenous peoples, although they often leave some land for their subsistence needs. Large-scale colonisation of formerly isolated areas, on the other hand, may threaten to turn indigenous peoples into minorities in their ancient lands. Eventually such programmes menace the entire land base of indigenous people, and therefore their economic, social and cultural integrity. The negative effects of colonial practices, as well as 19th century government-sponsored settling of European farmers on Indian lands in the Americas, should provide a warning to current schemes.

This process affecting indigenous peoples' lands is currently being carried out in Bangladesh, Belize, Brazil, Honduras, Indonesia and Peru. Resettlement, or transmigration as it is known in Indonesia, is a government-run programme to remove mainly poor and landless peasants from densely populated areas to the less populated regions of the country. Governments claim that the cultivable land in other areas is insufficient to support a growing rural population, and that the remote marginal lands of indigenous peoples are unoccupied or under-occupied and can only be exploited with an additional labour force. Colonisation programmes, because they address economic development issues, have attracted substantial funding from multilateral development banks, such as the World Bank and the Asian Development Bank. The World Bank's explanation for supporting the government of Indonesia's transmigration programme, for example, is that it will reduce the high population of the island of Java, reduce exhaustion of Javanese soils, exploit now unused lands and create necessary jobs.

The overpopulation claim is often used to justify resettlement programmes. In Indonesia, 60 per cent of the population of 165 million lives on the islands of Java and Madura, which account for less than 7 per cent of the total land area.[1] Population density on Java averages 700 people per square kilometre, compared with three per square kilometre on West Papua, the main target for resettlement over the next decade. Already more than 600,000 families (approximately 3.6 million people) have been moved from Java to the outer islands since 1964. However, the demographic impact has been insignificant. The population of Java increases by two million annually, and even by the most optimistic of estimates only 25 per cent of the island's natural population increase is being absorbed by transmigration. The demographic justification for resettlement has been discounted by Mr Martono, the Indonesian minister of transmigration. He stated at a meeting of the Inter-Governmental Group on Indonesia – a gathering of the major western donor countries – in 1985: 'Demographically, transmigration of people from Java does not mean very much, because the rate of growth on this island is high . . .'[2]

But is there any validity in the claim by governments sponsoring colonisation that the lands from which people are being resettled are overpopulated? There has certainly been a marked increase in landlessness and a deterioration of the standard of living of the rural poor of those countries with major resettlement programmes. However, the misery of these dispossessed peasants is not so much due to overpopulation as to the prevailing economic and political situation in the countryside. In Brazil, for example, out of a population of 138 million, about 30 per cent are officially classified as living in absolute misery. Despite this, however, there are 600 million acres of arable land lying unfarmed.[3] Leaving aside Amazonia where colonisation is now being promoted by the government,

Issues

the potential farmland available to each family could be 10 acres. Instead, 4.5 per cent of landowners in Brazil own 81 per cent of cultivated land. Such inequitable land distribution also affects Java, where a small number of rich landlords own a disproportionately high percentage of land. In Peru, where the government has sponsored a similar expansion into Amazonia, 1 per cent of the population owns 81 per cent of arable land.[4] In Bangladesh, where the government is resettling Bengalis from the plains in the Chittagong Hill Tracts, 60 per cent of rural households can be classified as landless peasants, yet 10 per cent of landowners own 55 per cent of farmland. As an economist has commented: 'The reasons why Bangladesh's agricultural sector fails to provide the population with food and productive employment are not a physical shortage of resources . . . The real reasons are the various inter-dependent distortions and constraints which originate from the economic, political and social structure and the concomitant choice of policies.'[5]

In addition, many settlers do not benefit from colonisation programmes. Indeed they may find themselves moving from a poverty they have learned to cope with, to an environment where subsistence is barely possible for them. There are a number of reasons for this. In general, settlers move to very different ecological systems, where methods of farming known to them are unsuitable. The Bengalis from the plains of Bangladesh, used to the rich soils of the Ganges–Brahmaputra, have no experience of farming the poorer soils of the Chittagong Hill Tracts; settlers from the dry north-eastern states of Brazil run into difficulties as soon as they try to reproduce their agricultural methods in the clearings of the Amazon rain forest.

Sometimes these pioneers have no understanding of the agriculture they will need to practise in their newly acquired land. A survey, by the Population Institute at Gadja Mada University in Indonesia in 1976, found that 45 per cent of transmigrants from Java had never before grown rice – the staple crop of most settlements.[6] In Indonesia, questions about the economic viability of transmigration have been raised by the World Bank itself. One consultant economist has commented that: 'None of the settlements had returns anything like those the World Bank said would be the minimum feasible

70

in its economic justification for the project.'[7] As a consequence, there are now indications that migrants are seeking to return home in a movement which has already been termed 'remigration'. The fact is that the soils in those areas selected for colonisation are not capable of sustaining large numbers of settlers, particularly people with limited knowledge and no sympathy for the environment.

In Brazil, colonisation has already suffered enormous setbacks. After the Trans-Amazonian Highway was built, a swathe of land 100 kilometres either side of the road, a total of 230 million hectares, was expropriated for colonisation. The Institute for Agrarian Reform (INCRA) began settling colonists in 1971. Its plan was to relocate five million landless peasants, and provide each family with a plot of 50 hectares or more. After clearing of the plots, soil fertility declined rapidly. Yields fell and marketing of the produce proved inadequate. By 1977, over one-third of the original settlers had abandoned their plots. As the smallholders moved away, large landowners swallowed up the abandoned land, at times even coercing the colonists grimly hanging onto the only asset they possessed. The opening up of the Amazon – to provide land for poor, landless peasants – has to date been by and large a failure.

In the state of Rondônia in Brazil's Western Amazon region, the population rose five-fold between 1978 and 1986, and the cleared forest increased from 4,000 square kilometres to 16,000 square kilometres. Before 1965 Rondônia had been very sparsely populated and Indians occupied reserves covering about a half million acres. Within 20 years the population of the state was well on the way to the one million mark, and all the available land had been claimed. But the flow of settlers had not ceased.[8]

If resettlement schemes are often painful for the colonist, they are an absolute disaster for indigenous inhabitants. First of all, the scale of the settlement alone is alarming. Within 20 years the government of Indonesia plans to move 6.5 million people from the highly populated central islands to the less densely populated outer islands. In the province of Irian Jaya (West Papua), inhabited by about 800,000 indigenous Melanesian people, over 80,000 transmigrants had been settled by 1984. But under the new five-year plan, 1985–89, about

100,000 families are due to be moved to the island. At this rate of migration, the West Papuan people will become a vulnerable minority in their own country before the end of the century.

In Nicaragua, under the Somoza dictatorship, some 120,000 Spanish-speaking peasants migrated to the eastern rain forest during the 1950s and 1960s, outnumbering the indigenous Miskito and other Indian peoples. Although land was plentiful and rich in the western parts of the country, the increasing control of land for commercial agriculture had pushed Nicaraguan farmers off their small plots. They became farm labourers or migrated over the central mountain ridge, bringing their cattle. Today, as the Sandinistas attempt to structure an autonomous government for the peoples of the eastern region, they are limited by the fact of the presence of a majority of non-indigenous settlers, who look down on the Indians and who, in turn, are resented by them. A project for remigration to the western region with offers of land titles may work. Meanwhile, no further migration to the eastern region is allowed. Most bothersome is the fact that the Spanish-speaking immigrants in the eastern zone oppose the establishment of autonomy for the region.[9] It may be expected that any area where such colonisation has taken place creates a time bomb and guarantees conflictive inter-ethnic relations.

In west-central Brazil, a grandiose scheme now under way will further increase settlement in Amazonia. The Polonoroeste is an integrated development project including road-building, colonisation and agricultural production. Over 60 million acres of land will be used, within which live 25 Indian groups with a total population of 8,000. The World Bank – part funding the programme – noted in an evaluation report that there would be negative effects, including conflicts over land and invasions of Indian reserves.[10] To its credit the Bank did insist on some protection of the indigenous population as a condition of the loan, although incursions onto Indian territory continue.

Even legal provisions by governments for indigenous territories may not be enough to ensure the survival of a particular community. In 1980 the Peruvian government announced a plan to develop one million hectares of its Amazonian region. The programme – The Pichis–Palcazu Special Project – would settle 150,000 colonists on land traditionally occupied by Ashaninka and Amuesha Indians. National and international protest against the project led to substantial changes in order to protect the indigenous inhabitants. The most important of these reforms was the titling of native land. In the Pichis valley all but five of the 40 communities were granted land rights. The average land base was 485 acres a family. However, despite the apparent generosity of the reserve, it represented a considerable reduction in the amount of land available to the communities prior to the scheme. Furthermore, the average amount of land suitable for shifting agriculture – the basis of the native economy – was 25 per cent less than that deemed necessary for basic subsistence. In other words, of the 40 native communities 20 already lacked sufficient land, while seven others were likely to encounter shortages within a generation.[11] In the case of Pichis–Palcazu, as with many other similar projects on indigenous peoples' land, officials failed to recognise the limits of the marginal land farmed by its traditional owners and perceived only its under-utilisation.

The lack of sympathy of most governments with the social and economic systems of indigenous people exacerbates the already disruptive impact of colonisation. There is little understanding of the highly developed inter-relation of indigenous people with their environment. Consequently, any agricultural practice different from the imported model established on the colonisation site is considered inefficient and primitive. In West Papua, dispersed indigenous communities practising shifting cultivation are being moved from their traditional lands and relocated in large settlement camps under the national administration. Frequently, these communities have no desire to leave their homes and are moved forcibly. Starting in 1986 the government of Indonesia plans to resettle 13,000 heads of family every year. If this programme is successful, the entire indigenous population of West Papua will be removed from their land and relocated in special resettlement camps before the end of the century. By such means the government will achieve its objectives of eliminating shifting cultivation and freeing for development the forests and other land occupied by indigenous people. As well as finding themselves a minority without political power, the West

73

Papuans will lose any economic independence they once had and become dependent on commercial and state agriculture and forestry for work. The Nicaraguan government developed a similar scheme in 1980 for resettling Miskito Indian communities which were so isolated that government services had difficulty in reaching them. The Miskitos objected to the idea and feared all of them would be relocated. Many took up arms. Nicaragua abandoned permanently the idea of forced relocation.

Large-scale colonisation, more than any other kind of economic development, raises the question of land rights. Officials and settlers alike have little understanding of indigenous economies. They see indigenous peoples as aimlessly wandering through the forest or arbitrarily clearing and planting. They do not perceive hunting as an essential part of subsistence. Yet it is the complex social, economic and cultural relationship of indigenous peoples with their environment which has allowed them to survive. What settlement schemes do is to discount this well established adaptation to the environment and replace it with new forms of land use, carried out by settlers from regions which are ecologically quite different. Moreover, tropical forest, as well as arid land, can support only limited human and animal settlement without destruction. What appear to be vast tracts of unpopulated or under-populated land is illusory.

Inevitably there are conflicts. Indigenous people see their land being occupied and, in their view, destroyed by the newcomers. The latter, however, only see the land as fertile, unexploited and unoccupied. These are irreconcilable viewpoints and governments make few efforts to try to bridge them. There are reasons for this. It may well be that an improvement in standards of living for the landless peasants and the indigenous peoples on land earmarked for development is the by-product of settlement programmes, but that is not the only purpose. Large-scale resettlement of the kind being sponsored in Peru, Brazil, Bangladesh and Indonesia – often requiring substantial loans from development banks – is also politically motivated. For the military dictatorship which came to power in Brazil in 1964, the opening up of the Amazon served as the panacea for the nation's economic ills. It offered a cornucopia of natural wealth as yet untapped; the relocation of landless peasants from the north-east acted as a means of defusing one of the most politically explosive regions in the country, without affecting the inequitable distribution of land.

In Peru, Belaunde Terry's civilian government which came to power in 1980 after 14 years of military rule and nearly a decade of economic deterioration, made expansion into the under-populated Amazon region a central part of its development strategy. In Bangladesh, the programme to move Bengalis from the plains to the Chittagong Hill Tracts serves both to reduce the political tensions arising from landlessness and opposition to the government as well as to undermine demands for local autonomy emanating from the indigenous peoples. In Indonesia the movement of Javanese to West Papua acts as a counterbalance to the independence movement which has been active since the annexation of the area in 1963. The Minister of Transmigration himself noted that transmigration sites are based on the Saptamarga model: settlement sites situated in politically sensitive areas and occupied by active or retired members of the armed forces.[12]

Resettlement on a large scale can be a tragedy, not only for indigenous peoples but also for the settlers who are led to expect improvements in their living conditions. Often both are disappointed by government promises. Poor landless peasants are brought onto indigenous peoples' land, often without consultation with the traditional owners. The two groups are set against each other; yet both are victims of government policy.

Indigenous peoples are not necessarily hostile to the idea of sharing their resources with other poor people, but they vigorously resist the use made of their land because, like colonialism, it seeks to impose an alien way of life on the self-contained society of a people.

Militarisation

> *'It is characteristic of the military mentality that non-human factors . . . are held essential, while the human being, his desires and thoughts . . . are considered as unimportant and secondary.'*

Albert Einstein, 1950

Speech by Lijon during her tour of the United Kingdom, March 1986:

'I am Lijon from Rongelap Atoll in the Marshall Islands. It is 100 miles from Bikini where many of the US nuclear bombs were tested in the 1940s to 1950s. On March 1st 1954 the biggest bomb, called Bravo, was tested at Bikini. We were not informed and we were not evacuated from our islands. The US took no precautionary measures to save us from this bomb.

'I was seven years old at the time. I was sleeping in my house and I only woke up when I felt the bright lightning in my house. We ran out to see what has happened. We were very afraid. Some people thought it was the war starting. Soon after, we heard big loud noise. A little later we saw a big cloud moving towards our islands. About 10 o'clock we began feeling very sick and something was itching in our eyes. Then came the fallout. It was white and we thought it was a white soap powder. Later in the afternoon I began feeling very, very sick. I had a bad headache and the other people in the island experienced the same problems. The next day the hurting got worse: big burns all over – legs, necks and arms. Late in the second day, Americans came back and took us away to Kwajalein for medical treatment and observation. We stayed for about three months. And then we were moved to Majuro Atoll in the Marshall Islands. In 1957 we were moved back to Rongelap because the US government said it was all right for us to go back to Rongelap.

'It was a few years later, in the early 1960s that we began to experience all the illness that we're having now. There are so many people back home who have suffered from thyroid tumours,

76

*stomach cancer, eye problems, kidney problems, heart problems
and leukemia. I have had seven stillbirths: some of these things
have no arms and no legs. In 1981 I was sent to US for to have my
thyroid removed and I have to take medicine for my thyroid every
day of my life. Every year the American doctors come to Rongelap
to examine the people and they say everything is OK; even though
we tell them we never feel any better. We have been worried about
our future and our children's future. In 1978 they had a special
study on Rongelap and they told us that we are never allowed to
eat any food from northern parts of Rongelap, only the southern
side we could eat from because it is only low level radiation. This
study made the people of Rongelap very scared for their future. So
in May 1985 we evacuated ourselves to an island called Mejato.
Mejato island is only one mile long. There was nothing when we
went there. We had to carry everything there on the boat. There is
not enough food on Mejato to feed our people . . .'[13]*

Since the Second World War the territories of indigenous
peoples have become areas of strategic importance to the
nuclear powers. Their lands and oceans have been used for
military exercises, nuclear tests and for the establishment of
military bases. Although the nuclear tests have by and large
ceased, the effects of those already conducted remain without
redress.

In the name of defence, the Warsaw Pact and NATO
countries have militarised the homelands of many native
peoples. In the little-populated forest and tundra regions of
Eastern Siberia and the Soviet Far East, the USSR has built
radar defence systems, military airfields and rocket-launching
sites, and also tested nuclear weapons. In Northern Canada, the
homelands of the Inuit (Eskimos), the USA has established a
string of Distant Early Warning Systems to identify incoming
missiles and planes. In Labrador, Canada, NATO has turned
the hunting terrain of the Innu Indian people into a testing
ground for supersonic aircraft and lethal weapons. The caribou
are now changing their migration and feeding patterns, and as
a result the Innu economy is threatened. In China's Gobi
Desert, the Turkic-speaking Uighur people allege that nuclear
tests have caused premature deaths, deformed babies and
poisoned grass and crops. In New Mexico and Nevada, in the

USA, nuclear and other military tests take place on the edges of Indian reservations. Only by mobilising public opinion were the Indians able to prevent these same areas from being used as sites for nuclear waste dumping.

But it is the Pacific and the Pacific Rim which have suffered most from the military build-up and 'preparations' for war. The atomic explosion on Bikini Atoll which caused the displacement of Lijon and other Marshall islanders was only one of many acts of militarisation in what has become known as 'America's Lake'. Since 1964 over 250 atomic and hydrogen bombs are reported to have been detonated in the Pacific region. Intercontinental missiles are regularly launched from the United States mainland into the Kwajalein Atoll in the Marshall Islands; and every two years the US Pacific fleet, accompanied by its NATO allies, engages in war games – the so-called RIMPAC exercises – which in 1986 included a continuous bombardment of the sacred Hawaiian island of Kaho'olawi.

The United States of America is not the only power laying claim to the Pacific. France also retains overseas territories for mainly geo–political and military purposes. It has occupied the island of New Caledonia for over a century, although in the last decade it has faced a vigorous independence movement organised by the indigenous Kanak people. France's fears are that, if it grants complete independence to New Caledonia, it will lose its control of the South Pacific altogether. By declaring 200-mile exclusion zones around its Pacific territories (French Polynesia, Wallis and Futuna, and New Caledonia) France lays claim to seven million square kilometres of ocean. The granting of self-determination to New Caledonia's Kanaks, it is feared, will stimulate moves towards decolonisation of French Polynesia.

Since 1966, Mururoa, on the south-eastern edge of Polynesia, has been the centre first for atmospheric tests and later subterranean detonations of nuclear devices. In the last 20 years, despite the health hazards, France has conducted 130 such tests, 50 of which were above ground.

What has been the impact of militarisation on the Pacific peoples? For some 500,000 indigenous people in the region, militarisation has resulted in the continuing abuse of their land.

Just as the French have been unwilling to give up their colonies in the Pacific, so the United States has retained the islands entrusted to it on a temporary basis by the United Nations following the Second World War. In addition, the United States has held on to Guam and American Samoa, which have been non-self-governing territorial possessions since the 1890s.

The Compacts of Free Association signed with the Marshall Islands give the United States the right to continued use of the Kwajalein missile range; the arrangement with Belau provides for the use of a part of the island as a military base. All these governments have undertaken to refrain from activities regarded by the United States as incompatible with its defence interests; the Northern Marianas has given the United States 'complete responsibility for and authority with respect to matters relating to foreign affairs and defence.'[14]

The militarisation of the Pacific and Pacific Rim has also brought about a deterioration of the physical conditions of the islanders. Reports prepared by the Brookhaven National Laboratory in New York since 1957 on the effects of fallout on the Marshall islanders confirm the serious hazards to health caused by nuclear tests. Radiation-induced diseases such as leukemia, thyroid cancer, stillbirths and foetus malformations have increased significantly in the vicinity of the test areas near Bikini and Mururoa. The environmental impact of the tests and the dumping of radioactive waste has been such that whole areas of the Pacific and its island clusters are now contaminated.

The military occupation of these small islands has also distorted their economies. In Polynesia, for example, defence accounts for 33 per cent of the economy and employs 15 per cent of the indigenous workforce. Once the islands were virtually self-sufficient in foodstuffs, but since Polynesia was chosen as a military base and testing ground, home production has suffered. In 1960 only US$3.2 million was spent on food imports; in 1980 the food bill had leapt dramatically to over US$650 million. 'We used to grow everything here, now we import 80 to 90 per cent of our food,' noted one islander.[15] Unemployment is high among the Tahitian workforce and they cannot afford imported foods. Slums, non-existent before the 1960s, now surround the capital. In addition, the militarisation of Polynesia has turned the islands – like others in the Pacific –

79

into prime targets in the event of war.

The transference of superpower struggles to peripheral regions has inevitably led to the embroilment of indigenous peoples. They have been drawn into conflicts and are the innocent and unwilling victims of both sides. They are the victims of ideological and political struggles, stimulated and sustained by outside interests. The hill people of South East Asia have been caught up in fighting since the Second World War. During the Vietnam War ethnic minorities were recruited by the Communist Party and by the French, and later by the United States armed forces. Hill people like the Hmong of Laos were made promises of autonomy, fed propaganda and bribed by both antagonists. They were set one against the other, often brother against brother. In the end they gained nothing for themselves. Over 200,000 Hmong are in exile or refugee camps, and those who live in Thailand are treated with suspicion by the authorities.

In Namibia the San (Bushmen), a small group of traditional hunter–gatherer people, have been recruited by the South African army. The government of South Africa has successfully exploited the traditional distrust of the San towards the majority pastoral Ovambo population and formed two battalions of the Kalahari Desert's indigenous inhabitants. The San are used by the South Africans to track down SWAPO guerillas. It will require an act of understanding and humanity by the Namibian people, in the event of a SWAPO victory, to recognise that the San are as much victims of South African government policies as other Blacks.

Miskito Indians were recruited into the war against the Nicaraguan government, beginning in 1981. Since their traditional territory overlaps the border of Nicaragua and Honduras, they were a natural target for recruitment, as well as being perceived as a threat to Nicaraguan security. In the process, their villages were leveled and around one-third of their population became refugees.

It is not only the conflicts between the superpowers or the struggles against the remnants of European colonialism which in the last 30 years have brought militarisation to the lands of indigenous peoples. There are also numerous movements for autonomy in the newly independent countries of Asia. In many instances, the peoples demanding autonomy or independence are indigenous peoples – often forest dwellers or hill people – who were marginalised during the period of European colonial rule. On the one hand, decolonisation in Africa and Asia and the international recognition of the rights of peoples to self-determination have inspired peoples' movements for autonomy or independence. On the other hand, the newly independent countries are concerned about creating a sense of national identity and the protection of their fragile sovereignty. They fear all secessionist threats. The result has been to bring independent-minded indigenous peoples into direct conflict with governments seeking to establish their authority over the entire territory. In practice, this has often meant that these indigenous territories are suffering 'internal colonisation' as part of a relentless policy of national integration.

In Burma, where one-third of the population belong to ethnic minorities, the Karen have been fighting for autonomy since 1948. As many as 300,000 civilians are alleged to have died as a result of the conflict and tens of thousands of refugees have fled to neighbouring Thailand to escape the bloodshed. In 1976 the nine main ethnic groups formed the National Democratic Front with the aim of achieving autonomy within a federal Burmese state. Since then the fighting has escalated, and the war has been carried to countless Karen villages in the hills.

The government of Indonesia claims the South Moluccas and West Papua – islands with Melanesian populations quite distinct from the peoples of Java, Madura or Bali – because they were part of the Dutch East Indies. When the Dutch withdrew from the region, the West Papuan people were not even consulted about the future of their country. In 1962 the Netherlands and Indonesia, pressured by the USA, proposed a brief interval of UN stewardship to be followed by Indonesian administration and a referendum on independence. The UN General Assembly approved the agreement. Until the referendum took place seven years later in 1969, numerous acts of repression of the independence movement by the Indonesian administration took place. When the referendum was held, the country was already in the throes of civil war. The plebiscite was not implemented on the basis of one person one vote; instead Indonesia arbitrarily appointed 1,025 representatives, including only one woman, to express the will of the people. Under the threat of imprisonment and even death, these delegates reportedly voted unanimously in favour of becoming part of Indonesia.[16] Since then the Free Papua Movement (OPM) has resisted what it claims is an illegal occupation by Indonesia.

Secessionist movements and rivalries between Big Powers are not the only cause of militarisation of indigenous peoples' lands. In countries such as the Philippines, Peru and Guatemala, indigenous groups have been identified by governments as communists and have faced brutal repression. During the rule of General Rios Montt in Guatemala and of President Marcos in the Philippines, the indigenous peoples of these countries were rounded up by the army and relocated to guarded camps. Their villages were bombed and their community leaders arrested, tortured and killed.

Militarisation, and all that it implies for the security and human rights of civilians, often has its roots in concerns and conflicts originating far away from indigenous peoples' homelands. Such action has already cost countless lives and threatens many thousands more.

Genocide

> *'Not only do most people accept violence if it is perpetrated by legitimate authority, they also regard violence against certain kinds of people as inherently legitimate, no matter who commits it.'*

Edgar Friedenberg, 1966

In 1961, a Paraguayan zoologist, L. Miraglio, wrote: 'In the villages near the Guayaki (Aché) areas, there are slave traders who organise veritable manhunts for these aboriginals. They catch a Guayaki family by surprise, murder the parents, and carry off the children to sell them.' A report in 1973 found the forest-dwelling Aché Indians close to extinction and still subject to capture and murder. Those forcibly settled on reservations were described as 'depressed, maltreated, tortured and in extreme ill health.'[17] In 1978 a North American human rights lawyer visited the reserves. He found all the children 'pathologically protein deficient' and noted that 'everywhere, there was a collective gloom of a people who had given up on life.'[18]

Finca San Francisco, Huehuetenango, Guatemala:

'On July 17, 1982, at about 11 a.m., 600 foot-soldiers arrived from Barillas frustrated at their failure to find a guerilla camp located in the nearby mountains and apparently ready to wipe out the village–estate of San Francisco . . . The colonel in charge of the operation ordered the people (Chuj Indians) to congregate in the centre of the village for a meeting. Even though the villagers noted that the faces of the officials were disturbed, they were not afraid because, on June 24th, the army had passed through with friendly words and without causing any damage. The soldiers scattered to call the women from their houses. Then they gathered the men and closed them in the courthouse and put the women in the small church . . . They then began to shoot the women in the church. Those who were not killed that way were taken to their houses where they were killed with machetes. Then, they returned to the church to kill the children who, separated from their mothers, had been left crying and screaming. They killed them by slitting open their intestines and smashing them against wooden poles. One eyewitness could see the horrifying spectacle through holes in the courthouse window and when for a moment the soldier standing guard opened the courthouse door.

'After killing the children, they began with the men – first the old men, then the working men and youths. They took them outside in groups and killed most of them . . . About 5.30 p.m., seven men managed to escape through the window of the courthouse, but the army noticed them and opened fire. Four lived and made it to the refuge in Mexico the following day. One was fatally wounded and died in hospital at Comitan.'[19]

Statement to the press by Mr Upendra Lal Chakma, Member of Parliament, Bangladesh, Dhaka, 1 April 1980:

'Armed conflict between army and resistance fighters has escalated recently, often with innocent civilians being used as pawns or scapegoats by the army. In early March, a 22-member

army patrol led by Major Mosin Reza, in the midst of a search-and-destroy mission in the Subolong Bazar area, Barkal Thana, Chittagong Hill Tracts, was ambushed by the Shanti Bahini. All soldiers were killed. Possibly in retaliation, a Captain Kamal of Kaokhali Bazar Army Camp requested tribal leaders and villagers to attend a meeting at the Bazar to discuss the law and order problem and to plan reconstruction work of several Buddhist temples, at 8 a.m. on 25 March 1980. At 9 a.m. of the same day, rifle fire suddenly broke out. The events during the confusion cannot be reconstructed definitely. However, by the end of the shooting spree – exacerbated by armed Bengali civilians joining in the military attack – an estimated 200 tribal men, women and children had been brutally murdered. The Bazar incident then spread with several Buddhist temples attacked, monks and nuns were mercilessly killed or wounded, and about two dozen villages in the union were attacked, some burned to the ground. The exact human toll is unknown but certainly exceeds 200. Massive migration of the affected tribal communities has taken place.'

These three cases – the killing of Aché Indians in Paraguay, the massacre of Indians in Guatemala and of tribal peoples in the Chittagong Hill Tracts of Bangladesh – have been described by indigenous peoples as acts of genocide. Indigenous peoples have also accused other governments – Brazil, Chile, El Salvador, Indonesia, the Philippines and the United States, for example – of similar acts. Many believe that all indigenous peoples are threatened by genocide or ethnocide. Genocide is defined by the United Nations as any act 'committed with intent to destroy, in whole or in part, a national, ethnical, racial or religious group'. Ethnocide is the condition under which an ethnic group is denied the right to enjoy, develop and transmit its own culture and language.[20]

The massacres of indigenous peoples are facts of history. The colonisation of the lands of native peoples in the Americas and Australasia took place at the cost of millions of lives. Entire populations were destroyed; indigenous cultures were debased and proscribed. In living memory of many are other, more recent, inhuman acts. In Brazil during this century, 87 Indian peoples are believed to have been destroyed. In El Salvador, following an uprising in 1932 led by the peasant organiser

Farabundo Marti, the authorities rounded up and killed 30,000 Indian peasants. All Indians were seen as subversive by the military. More recently, in 1982, the Pipile Indian villages were bombed by the Salvadorian army. Traumatised by the violence perpetrated against them, the indigenous people have abandoned their traditional culture and language. El Salvador is now practically 'de-indianised'.

During the Marcos period, villages of the Igorot in the Philippines were attacked by the army and air force. In West Papua, similar armed attacks against the civilian indigenous population have been carried out by the Indonesian army. In the Nicaraguan civil war, 1978–79, which brought the downfall of the Somoza regime, the Indian village of Monimbo was a particular target of aerial bombing.

But it should not be thought that the physical destruction of indigenous peoples is the only element of genocide. A senior official of the World Council of Indigenous Peoples has noted:

> Next to shooting indigenous peoples, the surest way to kill us is to separate us from our part of the Earth. Once separated, we will either perish in body or our minds and spirits will be altered so that we end up mimicking foreign ways, adopt foreign languages, accept foreign thoughts and build a foreign prison around our indigenous spirits, a prison which suffocates rather than nourishes as our traditional territories of the Earth do. Over time, we lose our identity and eventually die or are crippled as we are stuffed under the name of 'assimilation' into another society.[21]

When the Xingu Indians of Brazil were relocated, 25 per cent died from disease and homesickness. The forced removal of a people from their traditional lands has debilitating consequences for their physical and psychological well-being. Peoples able successfully to survive in one area will not necessarily be able to subsist in another. Diseases may be prevalent in the resettlement camps which did not exist in their homelands. The mere act of attempting to sedentarise and control peoples who are used to moving about with freedom can cause distress and demoralisation. A human rights lawyer visiting a missionary-run reserve found the Aché Indians broken: 'The destruction of Aché cultural values and their self-respect,' he observed, 'begins from the time a free Aché is captured.'[22]

In some countries the resettlement of the indigenous

population takes place on a nationwide scale. In Guatemala, the government has relocated most of the highland Indian population to army-controlled 'model villages' where their movements are strictly monitored. The army determines both the crops which are grown in the surrounding area and the social activities in the community. Men over 16 are forced to join 'Civil Self-Defence Patrols' to guard their village from guerillas and to denounce members of their own communities as subversives. The dislocation of Indian peoples from their homelands, their places of religion and cultural importance, and their forced recruitment into the government forces, serves to break down the sense of community. As the Indian spokesperson, Francisca Alvarez, has stated: 'The military seeks to destroy and shatter our cultural identity as Indians because the regime knows that our identity constitutes a part of our strength to resist and to organise.'[23]

In Arizona in the USA, 10 per cent of the Navajo Indian population is being relocated. They happen to be the portion of the Navajo still engaged in traditional herding.

To forcibly remove a people from their land, to deny them their culture and to destroy them emotionally and physically are, to say the least, acts of ethnocide. To attempt to assimilate and absorb indigenous peoples into the dominant society is effectively to bring about their disappearance as a people. Indigenous populations themselves certainly regard forced relocation and attacks on their cultural traditions as acts which jeopardise their survival.

The destruction of an indigenous people or their way of life can come in the guise of education and modernisation. At the turn of the century, for example, Aboriginal children in Australia – like Indians in the United States and Canada – were taken from their parents, trained to behave according to European values and put to work as domestic servants. However, the Aborigines and North American Indians survived as peoples and the attempts to 'breed them out' have now been abandoned as official policy.

In 1976 a French anthropologist accused missionaries in Venezuela of ethnocide against the Yanomami Indians. Like Pied Pipers, the missionaries were arriving by motor launch and luring the children away with sweets, cakes and presents. Once on the boat, the children were kidnapped and taken to a boarding school where they were subjected to intensive deculturisation. 'Everything Indian is devalued, scorned, set aside . . . . Children cried for their parents. Only busy adults, speaking an incomprehensible tongue came to console them.'[24]

But are these acts, which so threaten the future development of indigenous people, genocidal? The United Nations convention on genocide includes acts which cause 'bodily or mental harm to members of the group' and which deliberately inflict 'conditions of life calculated to bring about its physical destruction' (Article II). Are governments actively pursuing policies aimed at the eventual destruction of their indigenous populations? In some countries it is difficult to believe otherwise. In Guatemala both presidents Garcia Lucas and Rios Montt characterised Indians as subversive and instructed the army to treat all indigenous communities as potential or active guerilla bases. How many Indians have been killed by the army in Guatemala will probably never be known. In the first six months of Rios Montt's government, from March until August 1982, Amnesty International estimated 2,000 Indians and peasants were murdered. The US-based human rights organisation, Americas Watch, put the figure at 10,000. What is known is that all Indians consider themselves targets and many have fled their villages in terror. The Guatemala Conference of Bishops estimated that more than one million people have been displaced by the violence, and a further 200,000 have fled across the borders into the neighbouring countries. The Inter-Church Committee on Latin America in January 1984 called these acts in Guatemala 'the clearest example in Central America of genocide of indigenous peoples. Men, women, children and the elderly are tortured and murdered. Whole communities have been massacred.'

Yet governments accused of such acts have denied responsibility. Past acts of mass killings are not admitted, nor any reparations made to the survivors. However remote in time these atrocities might be, they remain vivid in the memory of the aggrieved indigenous.

The Paraguayan Minister of Defence in 1974 rejected the charge of government complicity in the death of Aché Indians. Governments ranging from Guatemala to Bangladesh blame the guerilla opposition and the prevailing conditions of unrest for the numerous civilian victims. It is, however, difficult to believe that governments are unaware of these atrocities or that they are unable to intervene and halt them. So why are governments failing to protect indigenous people adequately and allowing inhuman acts to be committed against them?

One cause of government action against indigenous peoples is racial prejudice. It is a vital factor in creating conditions favourable to ethnocide and genocide. The attitude of certain governments and the dominant society they represent is that native peoples are backward and primitive. The role of government with regard to indigenous people, it is argued, is to act as a civilising force. These arguments have characterised colonisation in the past, and continue to justify incursions into indigenous peoples' land today. The 800,000 inhabitants of tribal communities in West Papua are classified as 'Suku Suku Terasing' (SST) by the Indonesian government, or people who have 'less ability to perform adequately their social function'. Action to 'remedy' these alleged defective characteristics is contained within the Basic Stipulation of Social Welfare Legislation No. 6 of 1974 and Presidential Decree No. 45 of the same year which created a special office of the Department of Social Affairs to carry out government policy to:

1) Eliminate animistic traits and develop a state of monotheistic religion based on the belief in one Almighty God.
2) Develop aesthetic concepts and values in the art and culture to produce aspects which are in line with the values of Indonesian society.
3) Develop the communities' capacity for social interaction outside local boundaries, thereby eliminating tribal views and ways of thinking.
4) Induce the members of isolated communities to settle in an area with government administration and with permanent orderly sources of income.[25]

According to the Indonesian government policy, the indigenous languages are banned from schools and only Bahasa Indonesian is taught. There are no lessons on local history and even the use of the term West Papua is regarded as almost treasonable. The army is reported to have used coercion in the implementation of government policy. In the early 1970s, for example, the Dani people of the Balien Valley were forced to wear Indonesian-style dress and abandon traditional customs. Their rebellion in 1971 against this treatment was met by brutal repression.

The recent equally brutal measures by the Guatemalan military against the indigenous populations were carried out in the name of nationalism, which is often equated with anti-communism – a convenient formula used to justify repression.

The notion that indigenous people are inferior to the dominant ethnic group is used by governments to justify political and often military action. Young recruits to the army in Guatemala, often Indians themselves, are taught – according to their own testimonies – that Indians are a sub-human species and they are encouraged to abuse them. The former Foreign Minister of Indonesia, Dr. Subandrio, explained that the government policy towards the West Papuans was to 'get them down out of the trees, even if we have to pull them down'. The Governor of Irian Jaya (West Papua), Isaac Hindom, welcomed the massive transmigration of Javanese, claiming it will 'give birth to a new generation of people without curly hair, sowing the seeds for greater beauty'. Hindom is himself a Papuan.[26]

Many Latin American countries consider the solution to the 'Indian problem' to be the breeding out of Indians. In Bolivia where the Quechua and Aymara Indians constitute the majority of the national population, 'Indianness' is blamed for the backwardness of the country. No wonder that the immigration policies generally followed in the continent generously favour the importation of 'white' people. However, it is often the economic rewards of the land occupied by indigenous people which give rise to genocidal acts. In the Chittagong Hill Tracts of Bangladesh where massacres have been perpetrated by both the armed forces and the indigenous guerilla force, the government was accused by a Member of Parliament in 1981 of seeking a 'genocidal solution' rather than a political one. The attitude of many other governments towards their indigenous people can be similarly characterised. Likewise, in the policies of governments and mining, logging or other companies, economic interests often far outweigh humanitarian concerns. A leading mining tycoon allegedly favoured putting all Aboriginals together in a remote area of North-west Australia and doping the water 'so they would become sterile and breed themselves out'.[27]

Of course, such views do not reflect government policy in Australia, but they do show that even in democracies there can be talk of a genocidal solution to what is essentially a humanitarian issue.

The different kinds of invasions of indigenous peoples' land are prompted by economic and political interests which lie outside the control and, often, the understanding of indigenous people. Almost invariably they are causing hardships and difficulties which are of profound humanitarian concern. Frequently they may lead to the loss of life of the indigenous, or may erode their culture to such an extent that it ceases to be viable.

ACTION

7. National Action

Governments

'This government is giving my country a bad name.'

Tatanka Wotanka
(Sitting Bull)
Lakota Sioux Indian leader, 1887

Indigenous peoples throughout the world face continued loss of their land, cultures, and languages if present trends continue. Without effective guarantees by governments, these peoples will be overrun by mining, cattle ranching and logging operations, dams, colonisation schemes and militarisation. Indeed it is no exaggeration to suggest that the survival of certain indigenous communities and the well-being of most others will depend upon a dramatic change in government policies and practices. In some cases, ironically, the welfare of indigenous peoples is threatened by unbridled industrial and commercial development, allowed or promoted by governments in their areas. In other cases, such as the Andean region where 14 million Quechua and Aymara Indians make up the vast majority of the population, the present conflict has resulted from total neglect by governments of the region.

How ready are governments to move towards accommodating the demands of indigenous peoples? What action should they now be considering in order to rise to the challenge of this humanitarian issue?

Crucial to the welfare of indigenous peoples are the actions taken by governments and the inter-governmental organisations, especially the United Nations system. Governments represent the principal source of the present threat to indigenous peoples, as well as being the potential source of positive action to reverse that threat. Indigenous peoples are not prepared to remain passive victims of destruction, and many are ready to defend their communities and territories with their lives. The challenge to both indigenous peoples and

93

governments is to resolve conflicts in a peaceful manner and to find just solutions.

Some sociologists refer to the exploitation by governments of indigenous peoples' land and labour as 'internal colonialism'. They see governments as primarily responsible for the invasion of indigenous lands and for the subsequent damaging development. At the same time, it is to governments that indigenous peoples address their demands, as it is only governments which can guarantee any long-term improvement in their position. This Report looks at three directions which governments could seriously consider taking in responding to indigenous peoples: governments can greatly help to raise public awareness of indigenous peoples' perspectives and situation; they can enhance the legal and political position of indigenous peoples; and they can invest in programmes of social action to benefit indigenous peoples as well as curb private interests which seek to exploit indigenous labour and land.

Raising public awareness
Governments have a central role to play in raising public awareness of the situation of indigenous communities. Too often in the past they have thought of the indigenous population living in the country's backlands, ghettos and dilapidated reserves as peoples to be looked down upon, primitive and backward, to be hidden from view and left to dwindle in number and die out. Alternatively, they are seen as tourist attractions and romanticised. But in most states indigenous peoples are not disappearing. In some countries, they are the biggest group in society and often show faster rates of population growth than the majority.

Certain governments have already responded to indigenous activism. The government of Australia, for example, has recently acknowledged that their almost 200 years of dealings with Aborigines have been 'punctuated by dispossession, dispersal, disadvantage and racial discrimination'.[1] It has also recognised, clearly and unequivocally, Aborigines' prior ownership and occupation of Australia. These are great steps forward from the situation twenty years ago, when Aboriginal people were disenfranchised, suffered many injustices and did

94

not enjoy the full range of rights of other Australian citizens. While they are still the most disadvantaged group in society, the principle of their right to equal treatment is unquestionably accepted by the government. The same cannot be said about most indigenous peoples elsewhere.

Enshrined in the constitutions and legal frameworks of some countries are notions which take no account of the equal status of the descendants of the original inhabitants. In Brazil, the Civil Code describes the Indians as 'relatively incapable' and provides them with the kinds of rights afforded a minor; in Indonesia indigenous peoples are officially classified as 'isolated and alien' or 'isolated and backward' – descriptions which serve to justify policies of assimilation. In Thailand the declared policy towards the hill people is that they should be integrated into the Thai state. In the US, Indians are considered 'domestic, dependent nations'. Most governments' policies toward their indigenous people are based on legal norms which provide for their protection and eventual integration.

Underlying these assimilationist and paternalistic programmes is the notion that the culture of the dominant group, as embodied by the state, is superior to that of the indigenous. The relationship of the government to indigenous people is, therefore, often based on racial and cultural discrimination.

Governments are capable of transforming the climate of opinion through their public statements and attitudes. There are positive measures that can be taken. For example:

- Governments can recognise the prior occupation and ownership of the indigenous people of their land;
- they can acknowledge the damage done to indigenous people by colonisation;
- they can educate the public about the present situation of indigenous people;
- they can promote respect for their values, customs and ways of life.

Indigenous people can speak for themselves, but too often officials or 'experts' speak for them. Instead of consultation with indigenous people, government agencies choose to take advice from non-indigenous experts and advisers, or from hand-picked indigenous individuals. This disdain for the knowledge and participation of indigenous people only helps to confirm the erroneous idea among the general public that they are incapable of managing their own affairs. A negative stereotypical picture of the political and economic systems of the indigenous peoples is allowed to circulate unchallenged by governments. Indigenous peoples are by and large allowed to be thought of as indiscriminate destroyers of wild life or as passive, indolent and ignorant people. While such views prevail among the public and within governments, no policies of social justice can easily be implemented. A successful government programme of action requires the building of a consensus among the dominant group of the national population that indigenous people have been abused and exploited. It should also be recognised that they have a right to determine their own way of being and to choose their own representatives.

Enhancing indigenous peoples' rights
No expostulations on the part of governments, however worthy and progressive, serve any purpose unless real changes are effected in the legal and political situation of indigenous people. Real rights – whether to land, religion, culture, or political status, such as, for example, self-management – must be enshrined in constitutions and juridical systems of countries with indigenous populations.

Most important of all these rights, in the view of indigenous people, is the right to their territories and to customary land tenure and use. No peaceful solution to the problems presently faced by indigenous people can be envisaged unless governments put discussion of this right at the top of their political agendas. Without going into details here regarding the difficulties in relation to land rights, some key points need to be emphasised:

First, governments must recognise that in order to survive and develop, indigenous people need an adequate land base.

Second, it is essential to establish some mechanism for consultation on and discussion of the size, situation and legal and other dispositions of indigenous peoples' land.

Third, any body which is set up by governments to consider the question of land rights should ensure that the indigenous peoples concerned are fully consulted on equal terms.

There are examples of successful or partially successful land rights programmes. Some Australian Aborigines have negotiated with local governments and won ownership rights to large areas of land. The Kuna of Panama have managed their traditional lands with little government interference since 1938. The Xingu National Park in Brazil is, by and large, considered a model reserve for forest-dwelling Indians.

However, there are also many lessons to be learned from land rights legislation. The federal government of Australia, for example, has refused to pass a national land rights act and instead has made state legislatures responsible for this matter. In practice, this has led to great discrepancies in the legal and land rights situations of Aborigines from state to state. In Queensland, which has the largest Aboriginal population of all the states in Australia, the government is hostile to land rights. Consequently, no new lands have been granted to the Aborigines in the state and indeed the security of tenure of Aborigines on the few reserves which do exist has been diminished. Yet in the Northern Territory, recognised Aboriginal land accounts for nearly one-sixth of the state. In the USA, native Americans have struggled against devolution of federal trusteeship to the state governments, not always with success. When federal status is lost, the land base disappears rapidly.

Laws relating to indigenous peoples' land may exist, as they do in Brazil, but their implementation is slow or inadequate. Consequently, there are enormous technical difficulties in protecting Indian reserves. Amazonia is the world's largest rain forest and the monitoring of demarcated lands by government officials is a mammoth task. Yet even where incursions into reserves by settlers, ranchers or prospectors have taken place illegally and are well known, government has not always intervened.

Although certain governments – Australia, Canada and Nicaragua, for example – have introduced land rights legislation of some description and implemented it, they have resisted giving indigenous people unequivocal rights to natural resources. Resources are deemed to be at the disposal of the state and indigenous people have, on the whole, been given no rights of exploitation on their own behalf or a veto in the event of damage to areas of cultural or economic importance.

Action

The government of Australia has provided some limited rights to Aborigines in respect to the latter, but has denied them control over how and on what terms resources should be extracted from their land. In Nicaragua, the indigenous have a right to a large share of profits and are to be consulted in decision-making, but the central government owns the sub-soil resources.

Nevertheless, innovations have been made by the government of Australia. The handing over of Uluru National Park, in which Ayers Rock is situated, in 1984 and the terms arrived at by the Aboriginal inhabitants and the government are examples of future possible developments. The new Aboriginal owners, instead of having exclusive use of the park, agreed to lease it back to the government. They now share in the income generated from tourism to their most sacred site, instead of just being the object of visitors' cameras. Furthermore, Aborigines are a majority on the board of management of the park. However, similar demands by American Indians in the USA to have a say in the control of national parks that were taken from them, such as Yellowstone and Mt. Rushmore, have been denied. Indeed, national park land in the USA makes up the largest portion of land which Indians are seeking to reclaim.

There are a great many fundamental legal rights which governments need to consider. At the present time, indigenous peoples in most countries are denied a formal right to autonomy. Indeed the direction is towards greater centralisation by governments, rather than devolution of power to indigenous populations. The control by indigenous peoples over the administration of their communities has gradually eroded as their territories are reduced or absorbed more fully into the mainstream. They are also struggling for rights in other respects. For example, the language of the majority is generally taught in schools and indigenous languages are left to fend for themselves. The languages of indigenous peoples are recognised officially by only a few countries. Peru, for example, recognises Quechua as well as Spanish. Nicaragua recognises Miskito and Suma as official languages in the Eastern region. On the other hand, in Paraguay, the majority of the population, both indigenous and non-indigenous, use Guarani as the *lingua franca* but it is not recognised officially.

Government bodies created to defend the interests and promote the welfare of indigenous peoples have often had chequered histories. The Brazilian National Indian Foundation (FUNAI), for example, has recruited dedicated fieldworkers, but appointed senior staff with little knowledge of Indian problems. FUNAI, like official welfare agencies for indigenous peoples in most countries, is often subject to political pressures and vested economic interests. The Brazilian agency is directly answerable to the ministry responsible for security and which, for much of the last 20 years, has had a senior armed forces officer as its president. Similarly, the Bureau of Indian Affairs in the USA is a part of the Department of the Interior, where competition with powerful departments dealing with minerals and land creates conflicts of interest. PANAMIN, the Presidential Assistant on Minorities in the Philippines (disbanded in 1985), was headed by one of the country's wealthiest businessmen, who also had substantial investments in tribal lands. Any organ established by government for the benefit of indigenous people can ill serve its purpose unless it is autonomous and composed for the most part of genuine representatives of the indigenous. It also needs extensive powers to intervene on their behalf. Governments must resist the temptation to control or manipulate indigenous organisations, whether on the national or international level.

Governments remain largely indifferent to the concerns of their indigenous populations, even should they be willing to grant them wide legal protection or additional rights. With respect to the legal and constitutional changes necessary, governments must first recognise that the indigenous populations are disadvantaged and then establish ways of consulting them. The key element of the government's approach to indigenous peoples should be meaningful consultation and negotiation on equal footing.

Investing in a programme of action
The proportion of government spending set aside for the welfare of its indigenous population is in most cases negligible. Yet, increasingly, a significant part of the national wealth is extracted from the natural resources located on the land of indigenous peoples. Government-sponsored development

99

Action

projects dispossess indigenous peoples of their land and offer little or no compensation or participation in the income generated or employment created. Furthermore, indigenous peoples are greatly disadvantaged in education, health, housing and welfare generally.

The responsibility of governments must be to ensure that an equitable share of the benefits arising from development on their land accrue to indigenous people. The use of such benefits must be decided upon in full consultation with the indigenous themselves. It is equally clear that, unless more is invested in health, education (including instruction given in their own languages) and adequate welfare provision, indigenous peoples will not be able to maintain and strengthen their identity, participate on an equal footing in the national society, or properly defend their interests. Instead they will remain a marginalised group with little control over their own destiny.

The potential for long-term improvement in the situation of indigenous people is there, as shown by Australia. After decades of neglect, the government began to concern itself with the welfare of the Aborigines in the late 1960s. The Labour administration under Prime Minister Gough Whitlam set up a Department for Aboriginal Affairs and put substantial funds at its disposal. Much of this financial support was channelled through legal, health and welfare organisations established and controlled by Aboriginal people. The impact of this is only now beginning to be seen. What was unthinkable 20 years ago is becoming a reality; dozens of Aborigines are now practising lawyers and advocates of the Aboriginal cause. In 1985 the first Aboriginal woman lawyer graduated. In 1980 the Aboriginal Development Commission was founded and funded by the government – under total Aboriginal control – to provide grants and loans to Aboriginal communities and individuals. Since then community centres and Aboriginal schools have been set up, land has been purchased and entrepreneurial activities have been sponsored. Aboriginal people are still a disadvantaged group in Australia despite these changes, but few would deny that considerable improvements have been made by the government in response to Aboriginal demands.

What Australia, and more recently Nicaragua, have done in terms of social welfare serve as examples for what is

100

economically possible both in developed and developing countries. Two key principles in these programmes merit serious consideration by all governments responsible for indigenous peoples. The first is that, in order to improve the welfare of this section of society, governments must be prepared to give its welfare a higher priority and therefore invest more time and energy; the second is that indigenous peoples must be empowered to manage their lives as they think best, supported by their share of national resources.

Corporations

'Concentration of economic power in all-embracing corporations . . . represents private enterprise becoming a kind of private government which is a power unto itself – a regimentation of other people's money and other people's lives.'

Franklin Roosevelt, 1936

In 1982 a conference was held by indigenous peoples' and other concerned non-governmental organisations in Washington D.C. on the impact of transnational corporations (TNCs) on native resources. It was not the first such meeting – a working group to discuss the effects of TNCs on indigenous peoples' resources had been set up as part of the International NGO Conference on Indigenous Peoples and the Land in September 1981 in Geneva – nor will it be the last. TNCs have an all-pervading presence in the modern world, and the homelands of indigenous peoples are no exception. The 1982 conference brought together indigenous representatives from Australia, Brazil, Canada, Ecuador, Guatemala, the Marshall Islands, Peru, and the United States, including Hawaii and Alaska. All the representatives described the harmful effects on indigenous peoples of the activities of TNCs. All in all, representatives of 35 indigenous nations expressed their concern about the role played by TNCs.

There could have been many more complaints. Indigenous peoples inhabit some of the world's last frontier lands whose resources have not yet been fully explored or exploited. However, in the last 30 years there have been incursions into these lands which fall just short of onslaughts: forests have been cut down, mines dug, great networks of roads built and hordes of outside labourers brought in. Few indigenous peoples have been unaffected by this resource rush and most have been taken by surprise.

The world's major TNCs are invariably involved in the projects to open up and exploit these lands. Dozens of companies – ALCOA, Bethlehem Steel, British Petroleum, Rio Tinto Zinc, Utah International, as well as German and Japanese firms – have staked a claim to the vast mineral reserves on the 190 million acre site of the Carajas project in Brazil. Several thousand Indians and poor farmers are due to be displaced. In Indonesia's province of Irian Jaya (West Papua), the oil giants – Agip, Chevron, Conoco, Petromer Trend (owned by Oppenheimer of South Africa), Shell, Texaco, Total – have leased concessions in the coastal waters of the western tip of the island. The copper, gold, nickel, tin and other mineral deposits of the highlands are exploited by American Smelting, Broken Hill Proprietary, ICI, Kennecott, Newport Mining, Phillips Brothers, US Steel and various others. The transnational corporation ALCOA, through its subsidiary SURALCO, mined bauxite in Surinam in the 1960s which caused the forcible removal of several thousand indigenous people. In the 1970s the same company became involved in the construction of a US$400 million aluminium refinery and dam project in Costa Rica which threatens the homelands of Boruca Indians. Rio Tinto Zinc – one of the world's largest mining companies – has secured mining concessions on Guaymi Indian land in Panama, and through its subsidiary Conzinc Rio Tinto (CRA), on large areas of Aboriginal land in Australia as well as in Namibia.

In Guatemala – where the majority of the population are Mayan Indian farmers – the United Brands Corporation, better known as United Fruit, came to own two-thirds of agricultural land in the 1950s. In Brazil's Amazon region, several major foreign companies have acquired land for cattle ranching and speculation. Similarly, a US consortium including Swift Armour owns a ranch of 720 square kilometres in Eastern Amazonia. Numerous other North American transnational corporations – Caterpillar International, Massey Ferguson,

WR Grace, United Fruit, Gulf and Western, Goodyear – own a part share in the booming cattle ranching business. The German Volkswagen company holds a concession of 1,400 square kilometres and the Italian company Liquigas, the Japanese Mitsui, the Swiss De Buis Roessingh and the Austrian George Markhof also own parts of the dwindling Amazon rainforest.[2] Not all of these concessions are on land occupied by Brazil's indigenous peoples. Once concessions are made – rightly or wrongly – by governments, virtually no effort is made by the newcomers to ascertain whether there are traditional owners or not, and several clashes between the employees of these ranches and Brazilian Indians have been recorded.[3] At any rate, the non-indigenous peasants, poor and uninformed, are also unjustifiably displaced by such projects. In several countries, such as Colombia, Guatemala and the USA, the indigenous and non-indigenous have joined hands in their struggle against such incursions.

Even where development is government-sponsored, TNCs are often responsible for an important part of the financial and technical support. They are an indispensable component of virtually all major programmes to develop marginal lands because of their expertise, enormous resources and control of world markets. Even the smaller TNCs have turnovers which exceed the gross national product of some of the poorest countries. No one can question their capacity to influence governments, often significantly. So what has been the impact of TNCs on indigenous peoples' land and resources? And what code of conduct should TNCs be following?

The World Council of Indigenous Peoples has described transnationals as 'the most immediate and serious threat to the survival of Indigenous Nations'.[4] It argues that the lands allocated to indigenous peoples in the past were considered barren, marginal and unproductive. Now, however, even these lands are found to contain valuable minerals and resources which transnationals attest are needed to meet demand and ensure industrial development. Due to the influence of TNCs, indigenous inhabitants are increasingly seen as obstacles to progress and are forced to give up their land and natural resources.

In practice, the interests, culture and future economic welfare

103

of indigenous peoples are not considered the responsibility or concern of transnational corporations. Often, profits take precedence over humanitarian concerns. More importantly, in a conflict between a TNC and an indigenous people, it is the latter which may lose all – lands and resources – while the former puts at risk only a small proportion of its total assets.

In Wisconsin, USA, for example, Exxon has discovered one of the country's largest zinc-copper deposits on land claimed by Ojibwa Indians under the Treaty of 1854. They gather wild rice from a lake lying one mile downstream of the proposed mine site. Wild rice has been part of their diet for centuries, and is an important cash crop as well as a sacred symbol in their religious rituals. Large volumes of toxic wastes are due to be stored in tailing ponds 90 feet deep and covering an area of 600 acres. As the chairman of the Ojibwa, Arlan Ackley, pointed out: 'If Exxon's engineering is not 100 per cent perfect, the pollutants from the mine will ruin our wild rice lake. Exxon can move on when they have taken the ore out, but we have nowhere else to go.' Exxon's environmental impact report made only cursory mention of the Ojibwas' concerns, stating that 'the means of subsistence on the reservation' may be 'rendered less effective'.[5] The Ojibwa commissioned their own independent research and evaluation report when Exxon first announced its plans and were able to question the accuracy of the company's study. They were thus able to postpone the opening of the mine and insist upon further engineering studies.

However, environmental and social impact studies are not mandatory in many countries. Indeed, even where the law provides some protection for indigenous peoples and the environment, it is often by-passed or ignored altogether. Exxon's investment in the El Cerrerjon project in Colombia, South America, is such a case. El Cerrejon is one of the richest undeveloped coal fields in the world and the largest project ever undertaken in Colombia. The project is a joint venture between Intercor, a subsidiary of Exxon, and Carbocol, a government corporation. El Cerrejon is located on the lands of the Guajiros, Colombia's largest group of indigenous people. Although Colombia has laws to protect the environment and its indigenous population, Intercor did not submit an environmental impact study until two years after construction began.

By that time the report was a mere formality and could not affect the project design or the decision to go ahead with the mine.[6]

In recent years, however, there have been important developments both with TNCs and among indigenous peoples. The latter have successfully blocked some mining activities. Increasingly, they are using the courts and existing environmental legislation to force changes on or delay mining projects, as was the case with the Ojibwas in the USA. Alternatively they are ready physically to obstruct mining enterprises. When Roxby Management Services, a company owned jointly by British Petroleum and Western Mining Corporation, tried to extract uranium from a site at Roxby Downs in South Australia, Aboriginal elders sat down in front of the bulldozers and refused to move. The proposed Roxby Downs mine lies in the Sleepy Lizards Dreaming lands, an area sacred to the Kokatha and Pitjantjatjara Aboriginal peoples. The company's environmental impact study did not acknowledge the threat of damage to the sacred site, nor the Aboriginal peoples' request to have such sites protected. The protest by Kokatha and Pitjantjatjara elders, however, was joined by non-Aboriginal supporters concerned about the health hazards associated with the tailings – the waste material left after the processing of uranium ore. Although the Australian government did not order the closure of Roxby Downs mine, it bowed to the combined pressure of the anti-nuclear lobby and the Aboriginal people's movement, and cancelled mining of uranium on two neighbouring sites. The campaign by Aboriginal people to close down the Roxby mine still goes on.

There is growing recognition by non-indigenous people that large-scale resource extraction by TNCs on indigenous peoples' land may have adverse implications for the wider society. Indigenous peoples' struggles against TNCs have received significant support from trade unionists, scientists, church organisations and sectors of humanitarian opinion in many countries. Transnational corporations, for their part, are becoming more aware of the alliances of organisations concerned about their practices. They are also increasingly conscious of the role of public opinion. Rio Tinto Zinc has been criticised publicly by shareholders at its annual general meetings. Exxon has had shareholders, representing 2.5 per cent of its stocks, vote in favour of postponement of further investment in mining on Ojibwa-claimed lands. There were not enough votes to force the issue onto the agenda the following year, but sufficient to worry the president of the corporation. He agreed to meet the indigenous community. The public is increasingly concerned about the investment by major institutions – governments, pension funds, churches, universities, for example – in corporations with substantial interests in South Africa or the arms business. The fact that some major corporations are also exploiting resources located on the territories of indigenous peoples must begin to cause similar moral outrage.

So what code of conduct should transnational corporations be adopting to respond to these growing criticisms from indigenous peoples and the general public?

First, TNCs should be required by governments to undertake social and environmental impact studies to assess whether indigenous peoples will be affected by a proposed project. This appraisal should be as wide-ranging as possible and the fullest participation of indigenous peoples and other concerned groups should be sought.

Second, there is a need for all TNCs to be required to recognise the principle of negotiation with indigenous peoples. At the present time TNCs deal with governments directly and make decisions over the heads of indigenous peoples. Because they hold the land in common, the indigenous inhabitants very often do not even get the same legal rights as individual owners of property. The special situation of indigenous peoples is not acknowledged by TNCs and it has not been reflected in the Code of Conduct for Transnational Corporations prepared by the United Nations Committee on TNCs. When indigenous peoples have a historic claim to ownership and can show their continuing occupation and use of the land, TNCs should include them in the negotiation of terms and conditions of any project.

Third, TNCs, in recognising the importance of land to indigenous peoples, should also be required to undertake as far as possible to restore the land to its former condition. TNCs extracting resources from the land are only temporary occupants, while indigenous peoples are its long-standing guardians. The profits made by TNCs are sufficient to permit the allocation of a proportion for the subsequent restitution of the land in a manner which will allow indigenous peoples to continue to live there.

Fourth, TNCs should be required to respect sites of religious, cultural or economic importance to indigenous peoples. In Australia the federal governments' measures to protect such sites have obliged mining and other companies to comply with this practice. In the State of California in the US, similar requirements exist.

Fifth, transnational corporations should build into their project costs proper and adequate compensation payments to indigenous people for loss of land and resources. In certain cases indigenous people have received no compensation for the loss of their homes and means of livelihood; they have simply been removed from the project site. Proper compensation should reflect not only the material losses experienced by indigenous people, but also the social and psychological strains caused by relocation. It should be in a form which allows the community to remain together and retain its culture.

Finally, transnational corporations should ensure that indigenous people participate in the project and share in its successes. TNCs should accept the principle of royalty payments or make some form of leasing arrangements with the indigenous owners of the land. This should be negotiated under fair conditions which allow the indigenous owners to obtain a reasonable commercial rate. TNCs should also endeavour to provide employment and training to indigenous peoples affected by the project. In many cases, indigenous employees familiar with the area can be a valuable resource for TNCs. Likewise, TNCs should increasingly be ready to enter into joint projects with companies controlled by indigenous peoples. In this respect the joint venture between a company set up by the Pitjantjatjara people in Australia and Amoco to prospect for oil on the reserve should be seen as an example of a possible way forward. In order to bring about more equality in bargaining strengths, governments should set up a department to provide funds to indigenous peoples for the legal, commercial and technical expertise required in negotiations with TNCs.

Action

The profits generated by the major transnational corporations are gigantic. A substantial part of them have been made at the expense of indigenous peoples, whose lands have been usurped and resources exploited. Proper consultation and compensation and a respect for the places of cultural value to indigenous peoples are a small price to pay for all that wealth. Many consider it unrealistic to expect but, if TNCs voluntarily accommodate the demands by indigenous people for a share in the wealth created and ensure an adequate process of consultation with them, they may forestall the day when mandatory measures have to be taken by governments to curtail their powers.

8. International Action

Financial Institutions

'A bank is a place where they lend you an umbrella in fair weather and ask for it back when it begins to rain.'

Robert Frost, 1972

Many of the large-scale development projects in the traditional homelands of indigenous peoples have been funded by multilateral development banks. Foremost among these banks is the International Bank for Reconstruction and Development (IBRD), popularly called the World Bank, which was set up in 1945 to 'help raise the standards of living in developing countries by channelling financial resources from developed countries to the developing world.'[1]

The World Bank
The World Bank is an organisation of 151 participating countries, but one-fifth of the voting rights are held by the USA, and more than half are in the hands of only six major industrial countries: Canada, France, Japan, the UK, the USA and the Federal Republic of Germany. In 1985 the Bank provided US$13 billion worth of loans and credits. Its support for a development project is seen as a guarantee of financial probity by commercial banks. Thus, World Bank involvement in a project acts as a magnet for further loans. At the present time for every three US dollars it lends to a project, more than seven dollars are raised from other sources. The decisions taken by the Bank with respect to projects affecting indigenous peoples can therefore influence other investors.

Until 1982 the World Bank had no special policy for indigenous peoples. During the 1970s, it was criticised for its participation in projects which, instead of raising the living standards of the poor, were dispossessing indigenous peoples of their lands and causing hardship.

109

Action

In the Philippines[2] the World Bank as well as the Asian Development Bank were involved in hydro-electric projects and irrigation schemes in the Cordillera region. The planning process took no account of the wishes of the inhabitants living in the project area, the majority of whom were tribal people. If fully carried out, the reservoirs would have flooded valleys containing rice terraces built up over generations, submerged villages, cemeteries and other sites of cultural importance. The indigenous peoples of the Cordillera petitioned the President of the Philippines and the President of the World Bank and demonstrated their opposition in rallies and marches. Peaceful protest rapidly turned to violence. The armed forces intervened and many tribal leaders were arrested and killed; some joined the New Peoples' Army to fight against the government. Work on the overall project could no longer proceed. In 1975, the World Bank funds relating to the dams were reallocated to a power project in Manila at the request of the government.

Problems of a different nature arose when in 1981 the World Bank agreed to provide 28 per cent of the funds for an integrated development programme in the north-west region of Brazil. The land covered by the Polonoroeste project included the habitat of some 8,000 Indians whose interests were not fully taken into account. When the programme was announced, indigenous, church and non-governmental organisations protested that the Indians were bound to suffer. The World Bank was urged to withhold its funds until reservations were established. Some improvements were made by the Brazilian Indian Agency FUNAI, including the establishment of three reservations. However, the land was not demarcated and ranchers already settled on the reserve were not evicted. Once again, pro-Indian activists protested and the pressure on the Bank and the government resulted eventually, in 1984, in the departure of settlers and the proper establishment of the reserves.

It may well have been these two projects which, because they drew so much local and international attention, prompted the World Bank to consider guidelines for future projects in areas occupied by indigenous peoples. In 1982 the Bank published a policy document entitled *Tribal Peoples and Economic Development: Human Ecological Considerations*, and set out new operations procedures for project workers. These are positive first steps. The World Bank recognised, for example, that 'tribal people are more likely to be harmed than helped by development projects that are intended for beneficiaries other than themselves', a point often made by the indigenous. The Bank recommended that, 'whenever tribal people may be affected, the design of projects should include measures or components necessary to safeguard their interests'. Its operations manual stated that 'as a general policy, the Bank will not assist development projects that knowingly involve encroachment on traditional territories being used or occupied by tribal people, unless adequate safeguards are provided'.[3]

But, as critics of the World Bank have pointed out, the policy statement contained several contradictions and an underlying assumption about the inevitability of a Western style of development for indigenous peoples. For example, the Bank, while stating that it should not be financing projects which encroach on indigenous peoples' land, acknowledged that it should also help to 'mitigate harm and provide adequate time and conditions for acculturation'.[4] This seems to suggest that the Bank after all will support projects harmful to indigenous peoples. There is ambiguity about what conditions must prevail before the Bank can make a categoric refusal, and about when a positive response is conditional on reasonable protective measures being taken by governments. On these and other aspects of the guidelines set out by the World Bank, there is a pressing need for review and clarification.

Before the publication of its special guidelines, the Bank had been challenged by anthropologists and environmentalists for its support of Indonesia's transmigration programme to Kalimantan (Borneo). The Bank, it was claimed, was contributing to uncontrolled deforestation and widespread alienation of indigenous peoples' land. It was a badly kept secret that the Bank itself had doubts about the development value of the programme. Nevertheless, despite its own misgivings about large-scale programmes of relocation of populations and its stated policy on tribal peoples, the Bank agreed to continue to support further transmigration. This time it made a loan of US$160 million to assist in the settlement of up to 100,000 Indonesian families from the main islands to the province of Irian Jaya (West Papua). However, in 1987, it is reported that the number of families to be resettled was considerably reduced. The effects of transmigration in West Papua have been noted earlier in this Report and there is no need to repeat them here. It is obvious, however, that the settlement of such a large number of Indonesians on the land of a people who are Melanesian and, therefore, ethnically, culturally and linguistically different, is contrary to the spirit and letter of the Bank's policy guidelines.

Similarly, the World Bank is providing US$300 million towards one of the world's most grandiose water resource and hydro-electric schemes: the Narmada River project in India. The project entails the construction of a series of dams and the removal of hundreds of thousands of people, most of them indigenous. The project is opposed by environmentalists, economists and others in India. The communities living along the Narmada river do not want to move and it is likely that the project will generate controversy and opposition in the same way as the Chico River Valley proposal in the Philippines.

Why is the World Bank meeting such opposition in these projects? And what steps should it be taking to assist the economic development of indigenous peoples? In the first place, the World Bank, like many other institutions, does not directly consult indigenous peoples. Its guidelines are drafted by its own staff and suffer from lack of collaboration with indigenous peoples and other recognised authorities. For instance, the World Bank recently created an official post for the monitoring of its guidelines regarding indigenous peoples. A non-indigenous anthropologist has reportedly been hired.

The Bank does not carry out adequate social impact studies to assess the likely effects on indigenous peoples of projects on their land. In 1983, the consultant anthropologist to the Bank on the Polonoroeste project publicly complained that the preliminary fact-finding missions were too short and too luxurious and that consultation took place exclusively with the local élites. He went on to argue that the Bank over-emphasised the financial gain of projects, to the detriment of environmental and human rights aspects. At a hearing of the United States House of Representatives, the same consultant stated that he believed the World Bank was 'much more concerned with images than with the welfare of the native minorities'.[5] The same point was also made by another former employee of the Bank, who had assisted in drafting the policy statement on tribal peoples. She noted:

> When our proposals were accepted, it was because they enhanced the progressive image of the Bank and cost the Bank little. Where our proposals threatened the future of a project, or had major implications for Bank practices, they and we were dismissed as unrealistic and unpractical.[6]

The Bank also does not allocate an adequate part of its budget to indigenous peoples' welfare. This explains the relatively small allowance made for the fact-finding missions prior to a project and the low level of compensation for indigenous people built into projects. Even within the Bank, only a small part of the budget is set aside for monitoring a project's impact on indigenous peoples and the environment. Only five full-time professionals are employed in the environmental affairs office – the section of the Bank responsible for indigenous peoples – out of a total of 5,000 employees.

The World Bank, in its policy statement on indigenous peoples, has begun to recognise its responsibility. It has noted that there are approximately 200 million indigenous people, roughly four per cent of the world's population, and that Bank-financed development projects are increasingly taking place in remote, marginal areas where they live. The Bank, and other similar institutions, are likely to have an increasingly important role in determining the kind of development which benefits these regions. The Bank's decision to make a loan, and the conditions it builds in if it supports a development project, will be increasingly critical for indigenous peoples. It can collaborate in the destruction of indigenous peoples or it can contribute to their protection and welfare. It has taken some positive steps towards meeting the criticisms by indigenous peoples. This trend must continue.

It would be worthwhile for the World Bank to review its policy statement on indigenous peoples in collaboration with representatives of those peoples. It should carry out detailed studies where projects cover indigenous peoples' traditional lands, and co-operation in these studies should be sought from the indigenous inhabitants. The World Bank should substantially augment the proportion of funds destined for indigenous peoples when projects take place on their lands and substantially increase the number and authority of its staff working on behalf of indigenous peoples.

Other financial institutions

It would be misleading to suggest that the World Bank is alone in facing criticism from indigenous peoples, environmentalists, human rights organisations and others. Indeed, of all the multilateral and national development banks, the World Bank has probably been the most attentive to lobbying by pro-indigenous groups. The Asian Development Bank (ADB) and the Inter-American Development Bank (IDB) have both made loans for projects which have subsequently caused hardship to indigenous peoples. The Inter-American Development Bank and the US Agency for International Development (USAID), for example, have funded the Pichis–Palcazu project on the homeland of Amuesha Indians in Peru; the Asian Development Bank (ADB) funded the construction of the Kaptai dam in the Chittagong Hill Tracts of Bangladesh which displaced tens of thousands of indigenous. The London-based Commonwealth Development Corporation (CDC), set up to invest in long-term economic development in poor countries, was charged in 1984 by members of the British Parliament with complicity in human rights violations against indigenous peoples.

The CDC has invested in a palm oil plantation in the Philippines. Its partners – the transnational company Guthrie and the country's own National Development Corporation – had employed a paramilitary group to drive the local indigenous people from their land by threats and murder.[7] After a fact-finding mission by the Parliamentary Human Rights Group – an all-party body monitoring human rights – the CDC withheld investment in a second palm oil project in the area. However, the CDC's response to the well-documented evidence of serious abuses was slow and reluctant, and it was only after pressure from members of parliament that it took its limited action.

Of course, the CDC is not providing aid. It makes loans and must, therefore, put financial considerations first. But the multilateral development banks and national development banks are not commercial banks. They are set up for the purpose of assisting economic development, and they are – through their governors and directors – answerable to the governments and taxpayers of the rich nations. They have a responsibility to comply with international law and a duty to ensure that the poor are helped and not harmed by the development they sponsor.

International Organisations

'We the peoples of the United Nations determined . . .
– to reaffirm faith in fundamental human rights, in the dignity and worth of the human person . . .
– to practise tolerance and live together in peace with one another as good neighbours . . .
– to employ international machinery for the promotion of the economic and social advancement of all people . . .'

Preamble, UN Charter, 1945

In the coming years international and non-governmental organisations are likely to have a critical impact on the aspirations of indigenous peoples. They represent to a great extent the moral consciousness of the world. Their actions can create a favourable climate for governments to include indigenous peoples among their priorities. Some have done pioneering work in focusing international attention on them.

What laws have been established and what actions have the United Nations and humanitarian organisations taken so far? What measures and strategies are they planning for the future? And how far do they go towards addressing the problems and protecting the rights of indigenous peoples? There are many organisations and a large body of human rights law which can be instrumental in securing international protection for indigenous peoples and safeguarding their rights. Before taking up specific actions taken by international organisations, let us briefly review the state of international legislation relevant to the problems of indigenous people.[8]

115

Action

Within the United Nations context in general, there are nine distinct instruments which form a point of departure in discussing strategies for progressively developing the recognition of indigenous peoples' rights.

First, the UN Charter itself is an instrument which requires governments to promote 'human rights and fundamental freedoms for all without distinction as to race, sex, language or religion.'

Second, the Universal Declaration of Human Rights which is widely construed as a part of customary international law calls on all states to secure the effective recognition and observance of the rights of everyone to equality, non-discrimination, education, and participation in both political and cultural life.

Third and fourth, the two UN Human Rights Covenants of 1966 are important sources of law for indigenous peoples. Both the Covenant on Economic, Social and Cultural Rights and the Covenant on Civil and Political Rights stipulate a broad range of rights, including non-discrimination based on race, colour, or national and social origin. The Covenants also refer to the right of peoples to self-determination and to natural resources.

Article 27 of the Covenant on Civil and Political Rights makes a specific reference to minorities:

> In those States in which ethnic, religious or linguistic minorities exist, persons belonging to such minorities shall not be denied the right, in community with the other members of their groups, to enjoy their own culture, to profess and practise their own religion, or to use their own language.

Although indigenous peoples do not consider themselves minorities because they generally seek a wider range of rights and protection, Article 27 has been used successfully in individual cases by American Indians. For those from States which have signed the Optional Protocol, a fifth instrument, the complaint-filing procedure to enforce the Covenant and to have the case heard by the UN Committee on Human Rights is open to individuals or organisations.

A sixth UN instrument of relevance to indigenous peoples is the 1966 International Convention on the Elimination of All Forms of Racial Discrimination. The Convention prohibits and condemns racial discrimination, which is defined in Article I as:

116

... any distinction, exclusion, restriction or preference based on race, colour, descent or national or ethnic origin which has the purpose or effect of nullifying or impairing the recognition, enjoyment or exercise, on an equal footing, of human rights and fundamental freedoms in the political, economic, social, cultural or any other field of public life.

Indigenous peoples can informally lobby for their rights with the Committee on the Elimination of Racial Discrimination which supervises the implementation of the Convention, or file formal complaints individually or as a group if the accused government has recognised the competence of the Committee to hear the communication.

Specific mention of indigenous peoples under this Convention was made at the 1978 and 1983 UN World Conferences to Combat Racism and Racial Discrimination. The 1983 Conference endorsed 'the right of indigenous peoples to maintain their traditional structure of economy and culture, including their language'; recognised 'the special relationship of indigenous peoples to their land'; and stressed that 'land, land rights and natural resources should not be taken away from them'.

In its Programme of Action, the 1978 UN Conference also referred explicitly to indigenous peoples and urged states to recognise their right:

a) to call themselves by their proper name and to express freely their ethnic, cultural and other characteristics;
b) to have an official status and to form their own representative organisations;
c) to carry on within their areas of settlement their traditional structure of economy and way of life: this should in no way affect their right to participate freely on an equal basis in the economic, social and political development of the country;
d) to maintain and use their own language, wherever possible, for administration and education;
e) to receive education and information in their own languages, with due regard to their needs as expressed by themselves and to disseminate information regarding their needs and problems.

117

Action

The UN Conference also encouraged the establishment of international organisations for indigenous peoples which would enable peoples in different territories to develop cultural and social links. In fact, since the 1978 Conference, nine indigenous organisations have received NGO status in ECOSOC, bringing the total to ten.

A seventh UN instrument applicable to indigenous peoples is the 1948 Convention on the Prevention and Punishment of the Crime of Genocide. This Convention refers specifically to ethnic, racial and religious groups. It prohibits killing members of the group; causing serious bodily or mental harm to the group; deliberately inflicting on the group conditions of life calculated to bring about its physical destruction in whole or in part; imposing measures intended to prevent births within the group; and forcibly transferring children of the group to another group.

The 1960 Declaration on the Granting of Independence to Colonial Countries and Peoples is the eighth instrument which can be construed to have a direct bearing on the situation of indigenous peoples. Article 1 of the Declaration states: 'The subjection of peoples to alien subjugation, domination and exploitation constitutes a denial of fundamental human rights, is contrary to the Charter of the United Nations and is an impediment to the promotion of world peace and cooperation.'

A ninth international instrument that concerns indigenous peoples in general is the International Convention on the Suppression and Punishment of the Crime of Apartheid. It is concerned with, but not restricted to, South Africa. It establishes as crimes any acts which are calculated to prevent a racial group from participating in the political, social, economic and cultural life of a country, and any acts which are designed to divide the population along racial lines by the creation of reserves and ghettos. Both the UN Human Rights Committee and the Special Committee on Apartheid consider reports by States which are parties to the treaty.

ILO
The International Labour Organisation has been the pioneer among international bodies taking specific measures for the protection of indigenous peoples. It undertook studies on the

118

situation of 'indigenous workers' as early as 1921.[9] The ILO Governing Body established in 1926 a Committee of Experts on Native Labour in order to elaborate international standards for their protection. This process led to the treatment of the subject in a number of instruments, including the Forced Labour Convention of 1930, the Recruiting of Indigenous Workers Convention of 1936, the Contracts of Employment (Indigenous Workers) Convention of 1939 and the Penal Sanctions (Indigenous Workers) Convention of the same year. The question of indigenous workers was kept under review by ILO through meetings of experts and consultants. It should be noted, however, that all these efforts were geared essentially to indigenous workers and their integration and development within national societies. The Andean Indian Programme launched by the UN system in 1953 illustrates well this approach. It was managed by ILO with the collaboration of the Food and Agriculture Organisation (FAO), the UN Educational, Scientific and Cultural Organisation (UNESCO), UN Children's Fund (UNICEF) and the World Health Organisation (WHO). The programme was intended to facilitate integration and development and was initiated in Bolivia, Ecuador and Venezuela. It was later extended to Argentina, Chile, and Colombia.

In 1953 the ILO published its first comprehensive study of the working and living conditions of indigenous peoples. On 5 June 1957, it adopted a *Convention concerning the Protection and Integration of Indigenous and Other Tribal and Semi-Tribal Populations in Independent Countries* (ILO Convention 107). At the same time, ILO adopted a detailed recommendation supplementing the Convention, and setting out standards for the treatment of the indigenous people.

At present, the ILO Convention 107 is the only international instrument dealing exclusively with the problems of indigenous people. It contains 37 articles divided into eight parts dealing with general policy as well as specific issues such as land, conditions of employment, vocational training, rural industries, social security and health education as well as means of communication. The text of this Convention is attached to this Report as Annex I. The Convention has been ratified by only 27 countries including several countries with sizeable indigenous or tribal populations such as Bangladesh, Brazil, India, Mexico, Paraguay and Peru. However many countries which have indigenous populations – in Asia and the Pacific as well as North America and Scandinavia – are not parties.

The ILO Convention No. 107 of 1957 is the only international instrument which recognises the right to collective ownership of land. However, its original orientation was towards 'integration' of the indigenous into the dominant society and 'development' in the Western sense. Indigenous people strongly objected to the Convention's paternalism. In 1985, the ILO began the process of revising the Convention in order to make it more comprehensive and bring it in line with the evolving standards for the protection of indigenous rights. In 1986, the ILO organised a Meeting of Experts on the Revision of the 1957 Convention. The experts recommended unanimously that the Convention be revised urgently. The meeting was an unusual one for the ILO, which operates under a tripartite system with representatives of governments, workers, and employers, but has no provision for non-governmental representation. In organising the meeting, the ILO included two indigenous advocacy organisations as full members of the group of experts, and invited a number of other indigenous and advocacy organisations to participate as observers, with a great degree of flexibility in participation. The recommendations and conclusions of the meeting (full text in Annex I, following the texts of Convention 107 and Recommendation 104), reflect a wide consensus, including the views of the indigenous people themselves.

The revised Convention is to be considered by the ILO General Conference at its 1988 annual session and it is hoped that it could be adopted by 1989. The draft revision eliminated the integrationist orientation of the instrument. We believe that it would be most helpful if the adoption process could be accelerated, as well as the eventual adhesion and ratification by the greatest number of States, including in particular those directly concerned, be vigorously followed up. We also hope that the ILO will, at the same time, look into the possibility of devising a mechanism for the inclusion of indigenous representatives on a permanent basis, both for the revision and eventually for monitoring the implementation of the Convention.

The indigenous representatives present at the 1977 indigenous conference which first recommended revision of the Convention did well in disregarding the views of 'experts' who at the time thought that the Convention could never be revised. The indigenous felt that the 1957 Convention should be revised, and if not, condemned. The pressure exerted by the indigenous organisations and representatives played a vital role in starting the process of revision.

The UN Network
In addition to the specific role of ILO, a number of UN bodies are empowered to remedy the deplorable situation in which the indigenous people find themselves. Within the General Assembly, the Third Committee which deals with social and humanitarian issues, and the Fourth Committee which considers decolonisation issues, are appropriate forums for indigenous issues. But owing to the existing inadequacy of international legislation and the political constraints of inter-governmental debates, little effort has hitherto been made regarding indigenous issues in the UN General Assembly. However, in 1986, the General Assembly did act to establish the Voluntary Fund for Indigenous Populations and has included indigenous peoples in its resolutions on the UN Decade to Combat Racism.

The UN Sub-Commission on the Prevention of Discrimination and Protection of Minorities has been active in promoting the protection of indigenous rights. The Sub-Commission is composed of 26 independent experts who are nominated by member states of the United Nations and elected by the UN Commission for Human Rights. In 1972, the United Nations Economic and Social Council (ECOSOC) authorised the Commission on Human Rights to request the Sub-Commission to conduct a broad study of the problem of discrimination against indigenous peoples. A Special Rapporteur was appointed, and after considerable delay, a voluminous report was submitted in 1983. The report covers a range of issues, including health, housing, education, culture, religion, employment, land and political rights. In its conclusions, the report states that present international instruments are not 'wholly adequate for the recognition and promotion of the specific

121

rights of indigenous populations as such within the overall societies of the countries in which they now live.'[10]

The UN Working Group on Indigenous Populations

In 1982, the Economic and Social Council of the UN responded to the growing international activity by indigenous organisations by establishing the Working Group on Indigenous Populations, with five members drawn from the Sub-Commission. The Working Group is mandated to 'review developments pertaining to the promotion and protection of human rights and fundamental freedoms of indigenous peoples' and to 'give special attention to the evolution of standards concerning the rights of indigenous peoples'.[11] It reports to the Sub-Commission and its reports have been made available to the UN Commission on Human Rights which makes recommendations to the Economic and Social Council. Although it is not authorised to adjudicate complaints, the Working Group has become one of the most important forums for initiating concrete protective measures. Its meetings are attended by more than a hundred representatives of indigenous peoples, in addition to a number of governments, inter-governmental and non-governmental organisations. At its last session held in 1985, the Working Group decided to place an emphasis on its efforts to prepare a draft Declaration of Principles on indigenous rights for proclamation by the General Assembly. The Working Group has already considered seven specific draft principles (see Annex II of this Report).

The Working Group is quite unusual in the United Nations system, since it is open to all indigenous representatives and advocates of indigenous rights, regardless of their formal status and whether or not they are recognised non-governmental organisations with consultative status in the UN. Although the Working Group has developed a productive and flexible method of work, progress is exceedingly slow, mainly because it meets for only five working days annually. This is simply not adequate for the urgent and huge task entrusted to it. We believe that it should meet twice if not three times a year. It is equally important that at regular intervals, its meetings be held in parts of the world closer to indigenous populations. At the present pace, its work on the draft Declaration of Principles will take at least a half decade more, and its recommendations will take at least another two years before the UN General Assembly completes action. It is clear that the reporting procedures which the Working Group is at present required to follow in order to translate its recommendations into reality are cumbersome and time-consuming. The Working Group reports to the Sub-Commission which reviews and reports to the Commission on Human Rights which, in turn, reports to the Economic and Social Council (ECOSOC) which finally reports to the General Assembly. We believe that at least one of the layers of this reporting procedure could be eliminated without harm to the substance. Such simplification would also result in economy of time, energy and funds.

The Working Group's broad mandate allows it to receive 'reviews of developments', or testimonies from indigenous representatives about their situations. However, only one day in the present time frame can reasonably be set aside for this item. This is clearly not enough time for all the indigenous representatives who attend to make presentations.

The Voluntary Fund for Indigenous Populations, established by the United Nations General Assembly by consensus, exists for the purpose of bringing indigenous representatives to the Working Group. A five-member body administers the Fund and it includes an indigenous representative. However, the Fund has received very little in contributions, and only from a handful of governments. Governments, non-governmental organisations as well as transnational corporations and indigenous companies must be urged to contribute to the Fund if it is to be effective. Obviously, a more vigorous fund-raising strategy is called for. We believe that it would be useful if the mandate of the Fund could also be broadened to enable participation by indigenous representatives in other relevant United Nations meetings and even for organising meetings relating to indigenous concerns at regional and international levels. The need for participation by the indigenous seems all the more important to us in the light of a series of suggestions we make in the following paragraphs relating to other components of the UN system.

In the context of its work programme, we feel it would be useful if the Working Group were to initiate or encourage the elaboration of precise rules of conduct to be followed by the financial institutions and transnational corporations when dealing with indigenous lands or resources. In their projects and programmes, they should be obligated to take due account of the needs and aspirations of the indigenous populations concerned. Likewise, at the conceptual level, the Working Group should help clarify specific details relevant to the indigenous in the application of the 'right to development' as elaborated in the specific General Assembly resolution. We believe that, in the case of the indigenous, the 'right to development' has a special historical and substantive significance.

Both in the case of the UN Working Group and the ILO, the Secretariat and support services clearly need to be strengthened if adequate back-up is to be available to the efforts of these and other UN bodies.

The United Nations Educational, Scientific and Cultural Organisation: (UNESCO)
UNESCO has been responsive to the rights of indigenous peoples although its action has not been as intensive or widespread as it could be. Its procedure for specific human rights complaints relating to the field of education, science, culture and information allows for both individuals and organisations to petition. After a complaint is registered, UNESCO consults with government representatives and attempts to find a solution which is satisfactory to the government and complaining party.

In 1981, UNESCO organised an important meeting of experts on Ethnic Development and Ethnocide in Latin America at San José, Costa Rica. Participants included anthropologists, who have long been advocates of indigenous rights, senior government officials, lawyers and indigenous organisations from all parts of the Americas. The comprehensive final report on Indian cultural rights which was subsequently adopted declared that indigenous peoples of Latin America had been denied the right to enjoy, develop and transmit their own cultures and languages. Governments and international organisations were urged to take measures to guarantee these rights.

We suggest that the question of indigenous people should be placed on the agenda of UNESCO's Executive Board and General Conference in order to develop a coherent global strategy in favour of the indigenous peoples in the fields of culture and education. UNESCO should also start and promote special field projects at the state and regional levels for encouraging and preserving indigenous art, languages, traditions and culture. It should, in particular, support rigorous action at global level to put an end to ethnocide practised by dominant societies against the indigenous.

The International Court of Justice

The International Court of Justice at The Hague is another UN organ which could be of assistance to indigenous peoples. Technically, only States may be parties to cases brought before the Court, but in practice, other means of obtaining legal standing exist. For example, the UN General Assembly or the Security Council can request an advisory opinion from the Court. And if authorised by the General Assembly, other organs of the UN and its specialised agencies can seek advisory opinions from the Court. In addition, under certain human rights treaties, state parties may bring before the Court cases which concern violations of treaty obligations by other state parties to the same treaty. The Constitution of the ILO in reference to their Conventions as well as the Conventions on Genocide and on Apartheid specifically provide for such procedure. One suggestion has been made that the General Assembly request an advisory opinion from the World Court on the current validity of indigenous treaties with governments.

Other Action Within the UN Framework

It is important that the human and financial resources, as well as the influence of all the different organisations and programmes within the United Nations system be mobilised, within the context of their respective mandates, to support the cause of indigenous peoples. We suggest that the UN Working Group and ILO play the leading role in setting out the ground rules for such cooperation. Organisations such as the United Nations Environment Programme (UNEP), the United Nations Conference on Trade and Development (UNCTAD) and the

United Nations Industrial Development Organisation (UNIDO) could play a constructive role in making recommendations to governments in their fields of speciality for the benefit of the indigenous. Similarly, humanitarian work in favour of especially deprived groups of indigenous people in developing countries could emphasize their specific needs. Thus the United Nations Children's Fund (UNICEF), the UN High Commissioner for Refugees (UNHCR), and the World Health Organisation (WHO) could be called upon to elaborate, where appropriate, special projects for the indigenous people.

Certain activities of a more general nature initiated by the United Nations have already benefited indigenous peoples. For instance, during the Decade to Combat Racism, 1973–1983, regional seminars were held to delve more deeply into questions of racial discrimination. One seminar, organised by the UN and hosted by the Nicaraguan government in 1981, focused on discrimination against indigenous peoples in Latin America. It was the first extensive discussion on indigenous peoples to take place within the UN system. Keynotes of the seminar were the recognition that indigenous peoples have national identities of their own, which go beyond mere solidarity in the face of discrimination and exploitation, and that programmes of assimilation were not an appropriate response to marginalisation because they produce cultural alienation. The participants called for indigenous participation in the decision-making process on all issues affecting them. Support for the indigenous peoples' own organisations was seen as the starting point for effective action on their behalf.

In order to analyse and understand better the contemporary situation and needs of the indigenous, the UN Secretary-General or the UN Centre on Human Rights, with the support of the UN Working Group, should call upon bodies like the United Nations University (UNU) in Tokyo, the UN Research Institute for Social Development (UNRISD) in Geneva, or the United Nations Institute for Training and Research (UNITAR) in New York, to undertake special studies and action-oriented research on the indigenous. These bodies could seek voluntary contributions from governmental and non-governmental sources, including in particular the transnational corporations, to carry out their programmes on behalf of the indigenous.

Action at Regional Level

The Organisation of American States (OAS) has taken important action in protecting the rights of indigenous peoples. The Inter-American Commission on Human Rights, the main organ of the OAS devoted to the promotion of human rights, has recently heard six cases regarding violations of the human rights of indigenous peoples. The Inter-American Indian Institute, which is chartered by the OAS and based on the Inter-American Indian Treaty, demonstrated its great responsiveness to Indian demands by resolving at its 1985 Congress to allow official Indian participation in future meetings.

Regrettably, regional inter-governmental organisations in other continents – Africa, Asia and Europe – have hitherto tended to neglect the issue of indigenous people. This is partly because of the low priority accorded them in political terms and partly because countries have tended to treat the subject within the context of domestic jurisdiction and resisted or resented any effort to promote regional consultations and cooperation.

In order to increase awareness of the problem and to identify concrete measures that can be taken at the regional level, we suggest that the question of indigenous peoples be placed on the agenda of governmental bodies such as the Africa–Asia Legal Consultative Committee (AALCC), headquartered in Delhi. It has done useful work in the past on such humanitarian issues as that of refugees. Similarly, the Organisation of Islamic Conference (OIC), in Jeddah, could pay special attention to problems of specific indigenous groups within its member states such as Bangladesh and Indonesia.

In Africa, the Organisation of African Unity (OAU) is well placed to examine the question of the indigenous. In the context of the recently adopted African Charter of Human and Peoples' Rights and its implementation, it would be worthwhile to bear in mind the interests of the indigenous who have hitherto remained the most neglected and deprived communities. Europe, with its rich experience in the field of human rights, could also play a constructive role on behalf of the indigenous in the framework of forums such as the Council of Europe or the European Parliament. The Inter-Parliamentary Union could likewise be sensitised to indigenous issues.

In this connection, it is worthwhile mentioning the step taken by the Commonwealth Heads of Government which should be followed by other regional bodies. In their Declaration on Racism and Racial Prejudice (Lusaka, 1979) the member Governments of the Commonwealth recognised 'that the effects of colonialism or racism in the past may make desirable special provisions for the social and economic enhancement of indigenous populations'.

Indigenous representatives have received invitations and participated as guests at meetings of the Non-Aligned Movement Countries. However, no provision has been made for their permanent observer status, nor have any resolutions or statements emerged in reference to the indigenous. It is hoped this will change in the future.

Non-Governmental Organisations (NGOs)

Recognising that legal provisions, whether in international instruments or in national laws, are alone not enough to protect indigenous rights unless certain pre-conditions are met, indigenous peoples have effectively used non-governmental organisations to strengthen their position. NGOs, unconstrained by political factors which sometimes frustrate efforts of inter-governmental organisations, have been instrumental in raising public consciousness about the plight of indigenous peoples and forced the international community to take account of their demands.

Additionally, indigenous peoples have their own international or regional organisations to defend their cause. The following ten have gained NGO consultative status in the Economic and Social Council of the United Nations (ECOSOC): International Indian Treaty Council, World Council of Indigenous Peoples, Indian Council of South America, Indian Law Resource Center, Indigenous World Association, Four Directions Council, National Indian Youth Council, Inuit Circumpolar Conference, National Aboriginal and Islander Legal Service Secretariat and the Grand Council of the Crees (Quebec). Scores of others have emerged at regional or local level to defend their rights and promote their welfare at the community level or to serve as support and advocacy groups.

In 1977, indigenous peoples, for the first time, sat down with governments, liberation movements, and international organisations to voice their problems and request recognition and support. The occasion was the International NGO Conference on Indians of the Americas, held at the UN offices in Geneva. The Conference was organised by the NGO Sub-Committee on Racism, Racial Discrimination, Apartheid and Colonialism, of the Special NGO Committee on Human Rights (Geneva). More than 50 international NGOs, 38 states and over 100 indigenous representatives officially participated. The participants declared 12 October, the date of the arrival of Columbus in America in 1492, International Day of Solidarity and Mourning with Indigenous Peoples. Reinforcing this recommendation, in 1983, the Special Rapporteur of the Study on Discrimination against Indigenous Populations suggested that 1992, the 500-year anniversary of this event, be declared International Year of the World's Indigenous Populations.[12]

The Conference documentation was formally submitted by a delegation of indigenous peoples to the President of the General Assembly. The recommendations included a call for respect for traditional law and customs and for unrestricted rights of communal land and resource ownership. A recommendation was also made to establish a Working Group on Indigenous Populations in the UN Sub-Commission on the Prevention of Discrimination and Protection of Minorities. This recommendation, as we have seen, was taken up in the 1981 session of the Sub-Commission, and was approved by the Commission on Human Rights and ECOSOC in their 1982 sessions. The Working Group began its annual meetings in 1982 and, by 1985, had begun work on drafting a Declaration on the rights of indigenous peoples to be adopted eventually by the UN General Assembly.

The 1977 Conference further recommended that the UN Special Committee on Decolonisation hold hearings on all issues affecting indigenous peoples, with a view to establishing some appropriate form of UN trusteeship functions for indigenous peoples. A second recommendation was for an investigation by the UN Committee on Transnational Corporations into the role of TNCs in the 'plunder and exploitation' of land, resources and labour of indigenous peoples. Neither of these proposals has as yet met with success.

The Conference had also recommended to its own constituency to organise a meeting which would focus on the land and its relationship to indigenous rights. The NGO Sub-Committee on Racism followed through with this directive and organised the International NGO Conference on Indigenous Peoples and the Land, which was held in 1981 at the UN offices in Geneva. It is also organising, in 1987, a 10th anniversary meeting to assess the changes of one decade of international action in support of the rights of the indigenous people.

Towards international action

The organisation, as well as the content of recommendations made by these NGO conferences, originated from the efforts of indigenous peoples. Most indigenous peoples are not claiming the right to land illegally taken generations ago which is now in private hands. Nor is the majority seeking formal independence from the states in which they live. But almost all are demanding self-management over their remaining land and resources. In this context, indigenous peoples have developed great respect for and expectations of the UN, the ILO, and other international and regional organisations. The efforts of the UN Working Group to draft a Declaration of Principles and the process of revising ILO Convention 107 are important advances for the protection of indigenous peoples' rights. However, a process of thorough and regular consultation with indigenous peoples is essential for the successful outcome of the drafting process.

The central issues that must be addressed among the new standards are 'land rights' and 'self-determination'. Regarding the latter, the UN study, as well as the international conferences on indigenous peoples, have recommended that a special rapporteur be appointed to clarify the concept of self-determination as it relates to indigenous peoples. In light of the urgency of developing international legislation to better protect indigenous peoples from ongoing hardships, the UN and ILO should strengthen their human and financial resources in these areas in order to accelerate the drafting process and subsequent follow-up action.

Violations of indigenous rights are bound to continue even if new international standards are well drafted unless effective machinery is established to ensure their implementation. Since recourse procedures for indigenous peoples are largely non-existent or counter-productive at the national level, they must be developed further at the international level in order to influence national legislation.

As urged by indigenous peoples, recourse procedures must be devised within the UN system which take into account the threat to the very survival of indigenous peoples and their culture, and which include protection of their land bases and the right to self-management. One possibility, recommended at the 1981 UN Seminar in Managua, might be for the UN General Assembly to establish an office of International Ombudsman on the Human Rights of Indigenous Populations to monitor and report on the implementation of the new standards protecting indigenous peoples and to strengthen the possibility for the UN to hear complaints about violations of indigenous peoples' rights. The Ombudsman office could communicate its findings and recommendations to the Commission on Human Rights and, in urgent cases, directly to the General Assembly and to the Secretary-General.

It is incumbent upon the international community to rise to the humanitarian challenge posed by the problems of indigenous peoples. Their suffering must be alleviated and their rights as human beings protected if their just demands are not to escalate into violent action. Accelerated efforts to elaborate appropriate international legislation and, above all, establish adequate mechanisms to implement it will play a vital role in this regard in the years to come.

References

Chapter 1

1. United Nations, Document No. E/CN.4/Sub.2/L.566 of June 29, 1972.

2. United Nations, Document No. E/CN.4/Sub.2/1983/21 Add. 8, para 379.

3. United Nations, Document No.E/CN.4/Sub.2/1986/7/Add. 4, para 379.

4. Ibid., paras 380–382.

5. World Bank, *Tribal Peoples and Economic Development: Human Ecological Considerations*, Washington D.C., May 1982.

Chapter 2

1. Wilson, James, *The Original Americans: US Indians*, Minority Rights Group Report 31, 1976, p. 5.

2. Suter, Keith & Stearman, Kaye, *Aboriginal Australians*, Minority Rights Group Report 35, 1982, p. 11.

3. *New Internationalist*, July 1985, p. 5.

4. Riester, Jurgen, *Indians of Eastern Bolivia: Aspects of their Present Situation*, IWGIA Document 18, Copenhagen, 1975.

5. Wilson, op. cit., p. 6.

6. Suter & Stearman, op. cit., p. 11.

7. *The Times*, 19 April 1983.

8. Wilson, James, *Canada's Indians*, Minority Rights Group Report 21, 1977, p. 7.

9. United Nations, Document No.E/CN.4/Sub.2/1983/21/Add.5, paras 48–50.

10. Ribeiro, Darcy, *Os Indios e a Civilizaçao*, Editora Civilizaçao Brasileira, Rio de Janeiro, 1970, p. 237.

11. Colchester, Marcus (ed)., *The Health and Survival of the Venezuelan Yanomami*, ARC/SI/IWGIA Document 53, 1985, p. 9.

12. Government of India, *Report of the Commissioner for Scheduled Castes and Scheduled Tribes, 1979–1981*, Part 1, Twenty-Seventh Report, New Delhi, 1981, pp. 162–207.

13. Cf. Aaby, Peter & Hvalkof, Soren (eds)., *Is God an American?*, IWGIA/Survival International, 1981 and Stoll, David, *Fishers of Men or Founders of Empire?*, Zed Press, London, 1982.

14. Roberts, Jan, *Massacres to Mining: The Colonisation of Aboriginal Australia*, Dove Communications, Victoria, 1981, pp. 67–71.

Chapter 3

1. Cf. *American Indian Policy Review Commission Report*, US Government Printing Office, Washington D.C., 1977.

2. Roberts, op. cit., pp. 96–97.

3. Burger, Julian, *Tribal Minorities in Asia: The Indigenous Peoples of the Chotanagpur Plateau, Bihar, India*, report for CIDSE, February 1986, p. 40.

4. Myers, Norman, *The Primary Source: Tropical Forests and our Future*, W. W. Norton, New York, 1985, pp. 95, 97, 100.

5. India has, however, made some concessions to the tribal minorities of the northeastern states. In August 1986, for example, the government granted the Mizo people the right to their own elected assembly.

Chapter 4

1. Dunbar Ortiz, Roxanne, *Indians of the Americas: Human Rights and Self-Determination*, Zed Press, London, 1984, p. 33.

2. Sanders, Douglas, *The Formation of the World Council of Indigenous Peoples*, IWGIA Document 19, 1977.

3. *New Internationalist*, October 1983, p. 26.

Chapter 5

1. Cited in Wright, Robin 'The Yanomami Saga', *Cultural Survival Quarterly*, Vol. 6, No. 2, Spring 1982, p. 29.

2. Ibid., pp. 3–6.

3. Gjording, Chris N, *The Cerro Colorado Copper Project and the Guaymi Indians of Panama*, Cultural Survival Occasional Paper 3, March 1981.

4. 'Transnational corporations and their effect on the resources and land of the indigenous people', Australian Aboriginal Position Paper, International NGO Conference on Indigenous Peoples and the Land, Geneva, Switzerland, 15–18 September 1981.

5. Cited in TAPOL, *West Papua: The Obliteration of a People*, London, 1983, p. 40.

6. Langton, Marcia & Shea, Lyndon, 'Uranium Mining: The Impact on Aboriginal Life Styles', *Survival International Review*, Summer 1978, p. 14.

7. Eg. Iara Ferraz, 'Os Indios pagam primeiro e mais caro', *Ciencia Hoje*, November/December, 1982.

8. 'The Guaymi People and Cerro Colorado', paper presented by Chris Gjording for the Foro sobre el pueblo Guaymi y su futura to International NGO Conference, supra note 4.

9. Redhouse, John, *Uranium Genocide*, Institute for Native American Development, University of New Mexico, 1978. p. 3.

10. 'Multinational Corporations and the Indigenous Peoples of the Western Hemisphere', paper presented by the International Indian Treaty Council to International NGO Conference, supra note 4.

11. Roberts, op. cit., p. 132.

12. Statement of the Uniao Naçoes Indigenas (organisation of Brazilian Indians) to the United Nations Working Group on Indigenous Populations, Geneva, Switzerland, August 1985.

13. Pinto, Lucio Flavio, 'Mining permits on Indian lands announced', *Cultural Survival Quarterly*, Vol. 10, No. 1, 1986, p. 29.

14. Burger, op. cit., 1986.

15. Alexis, L, 'The Damnation of Paradise – Sri Lanka's Mahaweli Project', *The Ecologist*, Vol. 14, No. 5, 1984, p. 206.

16. 'The Social and Environmental Effects of Large Dams', *The Ecologist* Briefing Document, 1984, pp. 1, 2.

17. Centre for Science and Environment, *The State of India's Environment*, 1984–85, p. 119.

18. Alexis, op. cit., p. 206; Centre for Science and Environment, 1985, p. 119; Anti-Slavery Society, *The Philippines*, 1983, p. 92.

19. Anti-Slavery Society, *The Chittagong Hill Tracts*, 1984a, p. 32.

20. Anti-Slavery Society, op. cit., 1983, Chapter 5.

21. Centre for Science and Environment, op. cit., 1985, pp. 119–120.

22. Aspelin, Paul & Santos, Silvio Coelho dos, *Indian areas are threatened by hydroelectric projects in Brazil*, IWGIA Document 44, 1981, pp. 3, 5.

23. Caufield, Catherine, *In the Rainforest*, Heinemann, London, 1985, pp. 11–31.

24. Henningsgaard, William, *The Akawaio, the Upper Mazaruni Hydro-electric Project and National Development in Guyana*, Cultural Survival, Occasional Paper 4, June 1981.

25. Anti-Slavery Society, op. cit., 1984a, pp. 32–34.

26. Burger, 1986, op. cit., p. 35.

27. Writ of Petition to the Supreme Court of India, Lakra and others versus the State of Bihar, 1984.

28. Centre for Science and Environment, op. cit., 1985, p. 120.

29. *Akwesasne Notes*, (Rooseveltown, N.Y. USA), Late Spring 1982, p. 19.

30. Paine, Robert, *Dam a River, Dam a People?*, IWGIA Document 45, 1982.

31. Caufield, op. cit., pp. 26–28.

32. *Suara Sam* (Kuala Lumpur, Malaysia), October 1985, pp. 8–9.

33. IWGIA, op. cit., p. 96.

34. Burger, 1985, op. cit.

35. Myers, 1985, op. cit., pp. 154–157.

36. Burger, 1986, op. cit., pp. 20–21.

37. Centre for Science and Environment, 1985, op. cit., p. 91.

38. Turnbull, Colin, *The Forest People*, Book Club Association, London, 1974, p. 87.

39. Caufield, op. cit., pp. 37–38.

40. Myers, op. cit., pp. 94–95.

41. Friends of the Earth, *Tropical Rainforests*, London, June 1985, estimates that 45,000 square kilometres are lost through commercial logging; 20,000 square kilometres are lost through cattle rearing; 25,000 square kilometres are used for fuelwood; and 160,000 square kilometres are lost through slash-and-burn cultivation.

42. Burger, 1985, op. cit., pp. 19–20.

43. Centre for Science and Environment, op. cit., p. 51.

44. Myers, op. cit., pp. 128, 131–7.

Chapter 6

1. On Indonesia's transmigration policy see *The Ecologist*, Vol. 16, Nos. 2/3, 1986.

2. Proceedings of the Meeting between the Department of Transmigration and Inter-Governmental Group on Indonesia (IGGI), Jakarta, March 20, 1985.

3. *The Guardian*, 20 June 1986.

4. Cf. Caufield, op. cit., p. 39.

5. Vylder, S., *Agriculture in Chains – Bangladesh: A Case Study in Contradictions and Constraints*, Zed Press, London, 1982, p. 156.

6. Singarimbun et al., 'Transmigrants in South Kalimantan and South Sulawesi', Population Institute, Gadjah Mada University, Indonesia, 1977.

7. Cited in Otten, Mariel, 'Transmigrasi: From Poverty to Bare Subsistence', *The Ecologist*, Vol. 16, Nos. 2/3, 1986, p. 74.

8. Branford, Sue and Glock, Oriel, *The Last Frontier*, Zed Press, London, 1985, p. 145.

9. Dunbar Ortiz, Roxanne, *La Cuestión Mískita en la Revolución Nicaragüense*, Editorial Línea, México D.F., 1986, pp. 83–103.

10. World Bank, 'Brazil: Integrated development of the northeast

frontier', Washington D.C., 1981.

11. Swenson, Sally & Narby, Jeremy, 'The Pichis–Palcazu Special Project in Peru – A Consortium of International Lenders', *Cultural Survival Quarterly*, 10(1), 1986, pp. 19, 21.

12. Budiardjo, C. 'The Politics of Transmigration', *The Ecologist*, Vol. 16, Nos. 2/3, 1986, p. 113.

13. Cited in *Nuclear Free and Independent Pacific Bulletin*, Glasgow, Issue 4, Spring 1986, pp. 5–6.

14. Article I, Section 104 of the Covenant to establish a Commonwealth of the Northern Mariana Islands in Political Union with the United States of America.

15. Cited in Alan Rushbridger, 'Palms in French hands', *The Guardian*, 14 October 1985.

16. Osborne, Robin, *Indonesia's Secret War: The Guerilla Struggle in Irian Jaya*, Allen & Unwin, Sydney, 1985, chapter 2.

17. Cited in Munzel, Mark, *The Aché Indians: Genocide in Paraguay*. IWGIA Document 11, 1973, pp. 7, 24.

18. Arens, Richard, *The Forest Indians in Stroessner's Paraguay: Survival or Extinction*, Survival International Document IV, 1978, p. 3.

19. Cultural Survival, 1984, op. cit., p. 1.

20. Declaration of the UNESCO-sponsored meeting on Ethnocide and Ethnodevelopment in Latin America, San José, Costa Rica, 1981.

21. 'Rights of the Indigenous Peoples to the Earth', submission by the World Council of Indigenous Peoples to the United Nations Working Group on Indigenous Populations, Geneva, 30 July 1985.

22. Arens, Richard, *Genocide in Paraguay*, Temple University Press, 1976, p. 36.

23. Statement made by Francisca Alvarez, representative of the Guatemalan Human Rights Commission to the United Nations Working Group on Indigenous Populations, Geneva, August 1983.

24. Lizot, Jacques, *The Yanomami in the Face of Ethnocide*, IWGIA Document 22, 1976, pp. 19–20.

25. Colchester, Marcus, 'Unity and Diversity: Indonesian Policy towards Tribal Peoples', *The Ecologist*, Vol. 16, Nos. 2/3, 1986, pp. 89–98.

26. Osborne, op. cit., pp. 136, 140.

27. *Daily Mirror*, (London), 5 October 1981.

Chapter 7
1. Statement by the Government of Australia to the United Nations Working Group on Indigenous Populations, Geneva, August 1985.

2. Myers, op. cit., p. 138.

3. Branford & Glock, op. cit., pp. 193–203 and passim.

4. World Council of Indigenous Peoples, 'Transnational corpora-

tions and their effect on the resources and lands of indigenous peoples', paper to the International NGO Conference on Indigenous Peoples and the Land, Geneva, September 1981.

5. *Forecast of future conditions: socio–economic assessment, Crandon Project*, prepared for Exxon Minerals Company by Research and Planning Consultants Inc., October 1983, p. 316.

6. Hernandez, Deborah Pacini, 'Resource development and indigenous people: the El Cerrejon coal project in Guajira, Colombia', Cultural Survival, Occasional Paper No. 15, November 1984.

Chapter 8

1. World Bank, *Annual Report*, Washington D.C., 1982, p. 3.

2. Cf. Bello, Kinley and Elinson, op. cit., 1982, pp. 84–99.

3. World Bank, *Operations Manual Statement*, February 1982.

4. World Bank, supra note 3.

5. David Price, 'The World Bank and Native Peoples: A Consultant's View', Testimony presented at the hearings on the environmental policies of multilateral development banks, held by the US House of Representatives, Subcommittee on International Development Institutions and Finance, June 29, 1983, p. 8.

6. Watson, in Hayter, Teresa and Watson, Catharine, *Aid: Rhetoric and Reality*, Pluto Press, London, 1985, p. 274.

7. Catholic Institute for International Relations, 1982; see also Parliamentary Human Rights Group, *The CDC and Mindanao*, Report of a visit to the Philippines by Alf Dubs, MP and Colin Moynihan, MP, British Parliament, 21 September–1 October 1983.

8. A body of documentation and literature has developed regarding the rights of indigenous peoples in international law, which comprises a challenge to existing interpretations. Cf., for instance, Alfredsson, Gudmundur, 'International Law, International Organizations and Indigenous Peoples', *Journal of International Affairs*, Vol. 26, No. 1, Spring/Summer 1982, pp. 113–25; Barsh, Russel, 'Indigenous Peoples: An Emerging Object of International Law', *American Journal of International Law*, Vol. 80, 1986, pp. 369–85; Bennett, Gordon, 'Aboriginal Title in the Common Law', *Buffalo Law Review*, Vol. 27, No. 4, Fall, 1978, pp. 617–67; Clinebell, John Howard and Thomson, Jim, 'Sovereignty and Self-Determination: The Rights of Native Americans under International Law', *Buffalo Law Review*, Vol. 27, No. 4, Fall, 1978, pp. 669–714; Dunbar Ortiz, Roxanne, *Indians of the Americas: Human Rights and Self-Determination*, Zed Press, London, Praeger, New York, 1984; Sanders, Douglas, 'The Re-emergence of Indigenous Questions in International Law', *Canada: Human Rights Yearbook*, 1984, pp. 3–30; and, for instance, whole issues of law reviews: *Buffalo Law Review*: 'Law and Indigenous Populations', Vol.

27, No. 4, Fall, 1978, and *The Journal of International Affairs*, 'The Human Rights of Indigenous Peoples', Vol. 36, No. 1, Spring/Summer 1982.

9. Swepston, Lee and Plant, Roger, 'International Standards and the Protection of the Land Rights of Indigenous and Tribal Populations', *International Labour Review*, Vol. 124, No. 1, January–February, 1986, pp. 91–106; ILO, *Partial Revision of the Indigenous and Tribal Populations Convention, 1957* (No. 107), Report VI, (1), Geneva, 1987.

10. United Nations, Document No. E/CN.4/Sub.2/1986/7/Add.4, para. 625.

11. United Nations Sub-Commission Resolution 2 (XXXIV) of 8 September 1981; endorsed by the Commission on Human Rights by Resolution 1982/19 of 10 March 1982; authorised by ECOSOC Resolution 1982/34 of 7 May 1982.

12. United Nations, Document No. E/CN.4/Sub.2/1986/7/Add.4, para 633.

Suggested Reading

The following section is intended exclusively to facilitate further reading on the subject. It is not comprehensive and does not indicate in any manner the preference or otherwise of the Independent Commission.

Adams, Howard, *Prisons of Grass: An Indian History of Canada*. Toronto: Free Press, 1974.

Barsh, Russel and Youngblood Henderson, James, *The Road: Indian Tribes and Political Liberty*. Berkeley: University of California Press, 1980.

Bello, Walden, Kinley, David and Elinson, Elaine, *Development Débâcle: The World Bank in The Philippines*. San Francisco: Institute for Food and Development Policy, 1982.

Bennett, Gordon, *Aboriginal Rights in International Law*. London: Royal Anthropological Institute of Great Britain and Ireland, 1978.

Burger, Julian, *Report from the Frontier: The State of the World's Indigenous Peoples*. London: Zed Press, 1987.

Deloria, Jr., Vine, *Behind the Trail of Broken Treaties*. New York: Dell Publishers, 1974.

Denevan, William M, (ed.), *The Native Population of the Americas in 1492*. Madison: University of Wisconsin Press, 1976.

Dunbar Ortiz, Roxanne, *Indians of the Americas: Human Rights and Self-determination*. London: Zed Books, 1984.

Ismagilova, Rosa, *Ethnic Problems of Tropical Africa: Can they be Solved?* Moscow: Progress Publishers, 1978.

International Labour Office, *Partial Revision of the Indigenous and Tribal Populations Convention*, 1957 (No. 107), Report VI (1), Geneva, 1987.

Kuper, Leo, *The Prevention of Genocide*. New Haven: Yale University Press, 1985.

Lan-Phuong, Hoang, 'Ethnic Diversity and National Integration: The Vietnamese Experience', *International Journal of Asian Studies*.

Paris: UNESCO (1981) 61–87.

Lillich, Richard, and Hannum, Hurst, 'The Concept of Autonomy in International Law', *The American Journal of International Law* 74:4 (Oct. 1980) pp. 858–89.

Mörner, Magnus, *Race Mixture in the History of Latin America.* New York: Little, Brown and Company, 1967.

Mowat, Farley, *People of the Deer.* New York: Pyramid Books, 1968; and *The Siberians.* New York: Penguin Books, 1972.

Reno, Phillip, *Mother Earth, Father Sky and Economic Development: Navajo Resources and their Use.* Albuquerque: University of New Mexico Press, 1981.

Roberts, Jan, *Massacres to Mining: The Colonisation of Aboriginal Australia.* Victoria, Australia: Dove Communications, 1981.

Sachchidananda and Mandal, B. B. *Industrialisation and Social Disorganisation: A Study of Tribals in Bihar.* New Delhi: Concept Publishing Company, 1985.

Stavenhagen, Rodolfo, *Problems and Prospects of Multi-Ethnic States.* Tokyo: UN University, 1986.

Swepston, Lee and Plant, Roger, 'International Standards and the Protection of the Land Rights of Indigenous and Tribal Populations', *International Labour Review* 124:1 (Jan.–Feb. 1986) 91–106.

UNESCO, *Trends in Ethnic Group Relations in Asia and Oceania.* Paris: UNESCO, 1979.

United Nations, *Study on the Rights of Persons Belonging to Ethnic, Religious and Linguistic Minorities.* (Francesco Capotorti, Special Rapporteur of the Sub-Commission on Prevention of Discrimination and Protection of Minorities) (E/CN.4/Sub.2./384/Rev.1) New York: UNO, 1979.

United Nations, *The Right to Self-Determination.* (Hector Gros Espiell, Special Rapporteur of the Sub-Commission on Prevention of Discrimination and Protection of Minorities) (E/CN.4/Sub.2/405 /Rev.1) New York: UNO, 1980.

United Nations, *The Right to Self-Determination.* (Aureliu Cristescu, Special Rapporteur of the Sub-Commission on Prevention of Discrimination and Protection of Minorities) (E/CN.4/Sub.2/404/ Rev.1) New York: UNO, 1981.

United Nations, *Study of the Problem of Discrimination against Indigenous Populations.* (José R. Martinez Cobo, Special Rapporteur of the Sub-Commission on Prevention of Discrimination and Protection of Minorities) E/CN.4/Sub.2/ 1986/7 and Add. 1–4. Geneva: UNO, 1972–83.

Uvachan, V. N., *The Peoples of the North and their Road to Socialism.* Moscow: Progress Publishers, 1975.

Valkeapää, Nils-Aslak, *Greetings from Lappland: The Sami – Europe's*

Forgotten People. London: Zed Press, 1983.

World Bank, *Tribal Peoples and Economic Development: Human Ecological Considerations.* Washington D.C., May 1982.

World Council of Churches, *The Situation of the Indian in South America*, Bern, Switzerland: Ethnological Institute, 1972.

The following indigenous and other organisations publish information on indigenous issues:

Akwesasne Notes (Mohawk Nation, New York).

Anthropology Resource Centre (Boston, Massachusetts, USA).

Anti-Slavery Society.

CADAL, (Metropolitan University, Mexico City).

Cultural Survival (Cambridge, Massachusetts, USA).

Indigenous World Association (San Francisco, California, USA).

International Indian Treaty Council (San Francisco, California, USA).

International Working Group on Indigenous Affairs (Copenhagen, Denmark).

Inuit Circumpolar Conference (Canada).

Minority Rights Group (London, UK).

South American Indian Council (CISA, Lima, Peru).

Survival International (London, UK).

Annex I:

I.L.O. Convention 107, Recommendation 104, and
Conclusions of the Meeting of Experts, 1987

I.L.O. Convention 107

CONVENTION CONCERNING THE PROTECTION AND INTEGRATION OF INDIGENOUS AND OTHER TRIBAL AND SEMI-TRIBAL POPULATIONS IN INDEPENDENT COUNTRIES

The General Conference of the International Labour Organisation,

Having been convened at Geneva by the Governing Body of the International Labour Office, and having met in its Fortieth Session on 5 June 1957, and

Having decided upon the adoption of certain proposals with regard to the protection and integration of indigenous and other tribal and semi-tribal populations in independent countries, which is the sixth item on the agenda of the session, and

Having determined that these proposals shall take the form of an international Convention, and

Considering that the Declaration of Philadelphia affirms that all human beings have the right to pursue both their material well-being and their spiritual development in conditions of freedom and dignity, of economic security and equal opportunity, and

Considering that there exist in various independent countries indigenous and other tribal and semi-tribal populations which are not yet integrated into the national community and whose social, economic or cultural situation hinders them from benefiting fully from the rights and advantages enjoyed by other elements of the population, and

Considering it desirable both for humanitarian reasons and in the interest of the countries concerned to promote continued action to improve the living and working conditions of these populations by simultaneous action in respect of all the factors which have hitherto prevented them from sharing fully in the progress of the national community of which they form part, and

Considering that the adoption of general international standards on the subject will facilitate action to assure the protection of the populations concerned, their progressive integration into their respective national communities, and the improvement of their living and working conditions, and

Noting that these standards have been framed with the co-operation of the United Nations, the Food and Agriculture Organisation of the United Nations, the United Nations Educational, Scientific and Cultural Organisation and the World Health Organisation, at appropriate levels and in their respective fields, and that it is proposed to seek their continuing co-operation in promoting and securing the application of these standards,

adopts this twenty-sixth day of June of the year one thousand nine hundred and fifty-seven the following Convention, which may be cited as the Indigenous and Tribal Populations Convention, 1957:

PART I. GENERAL POLICY

Article 1

1. This Convention applies to—

(a) members of tribal or semi-tribal populations in independent countries whose social and economic conditions are at a less advanced stage than the stage reached by the other sections of the national community, and whose status is regulated wholly or partially by their own customs or traditions or by special laws or regulations;

(b) members of tribal or semi-tribal populations in independent countries which are regarded as indigenous on account of their descent from the populations which inhabited the country, or a geographical region to which the country belongs, at the time of conquest or colonisation and which, irrespective of their legal

143

status, live more in conformity with the social, economic and cultural institutions of that time than with the institutions of the nation to which they belong.

2. For the purposes of this Convention, the term 'semi-tribal' includes groups and persons who, although they are in the process of losing their tribal characteristics, are not yet integrated into the national community.

3. The indigenous and other tribal or semi-tribal populations mentioned in paragraphs 1 and 2 of this Article are referred to hereinafter as 'the populations concerned'.

Article 2

1. Governments shall have the primary responsibility for developing co-ordinated and systematic action for the protection of the populations concerned and their progressive integration into the life of their respective countries.

2. Such action shall include measures for—

(a) enabling the said populations to benefit on an equal footing from the rights and opportunities which national laws or regulations grant to the other elements of the population;

(b) promoting the social, economic and cultural development of these populations and raising their standard of living;

(c) creating possibilities of national integration to the exclusion of measures tending towards the artificial assimilation of these populations.

3. The primary objective of all such action shall be the fostering of individual dignity, and the advancement of individual usefulness and initiative.

4. Recourse to force or coercion as a means of promoting the integration of these populations into the national community shall be excluded.

Article 3

1. So long as the social, economic and cultural conditions of the populations concerned prevent them from enjoying the benefits of the general laws of the country to which they belong, special measures

shall be adopted for the protection of the institutions, persons, property and labour of these populations.

2. Care shall be taken to ensure that such special measures of protection—

(a) are not used as a means of creating or prolonging a state of segregation; and
(b) will be continued only so long as there is need for special protection and only to the extent that such protection is necessary.

3. Enjoyment of the general rights of citizenship, without discrimination, shall not be prejudiced in any way by such special measures of protection.

Article 4

In applying the provisions of this Convention relating to the integration of the populations concerned—

(a) due account shall be taken of the cultural and religious values and of the forms of social control existing among these populations, and of the nature of the problems which face them both as groups and as individuals when they undergo social and economic change;
(b) the danger involved in disrupting the values and institutions of the said populations unless they can be replaced by appropriate substitutes which the groups concerned are willing to accept shall be recognised;
(c) policies aimed at mitigating the difficulties experienced by these populations in adjusting themselves to new conditions of life and work shall be adopted.

Article 5

In applying the provisions of this Convention relating to the protection and integration of the populations concerned, governments shall—

(a) seek the collaboration of these populations and of their representatives;
(b) provide these populations with opportunities for the full development of their initiative;
(c) stimulate by all possible means the development among these populations of civil liberties and the establishment of or participation in elective institutions.

145

Article 6

The improvement of the conditions of life and work and level of education of the populations concerned shall be given high priority in plans for the over-all economic development of areas inhabited by these populations. Special projects for economic development of the areas in question shall also be so designed as to promote such improvement.

Article 7

1. In defining the rights and duties of the populations concerned regard shall be had to their customary laws.

2. These populations shall be allowed to retain their own customs and institutions where these are not incompatible with the national legal system or the objectives of integration programmes.

3. The application of the preceding paragraphs of this Article shall not prevent members of these populations from exercising, according to their individual capacity, the rights granted to all citizens and from assuming the corresponding duties.

Article 8

To the extent consistent with the interests of the national community and with the national legal system—

(a) the methods of social control practised by the populations concerned shall be used as far as possible for dealing with crimes or offences committed by members of these populations;

(b) where use of such methods of social control is not feasible, the customs of these populations in regard to penal matters shall be borne in mind by the authorities and courts dealing with such cases.

Article 9

Except in cases prescribed by law for all citizens the exaction from the members of the populations concerned of compulsory personal services in any form, whether paid or unpaid, shall be prohibited and punishable by law.

Article 10

1. Persons belonging to the populations concerned shall be specially safeguarded against the improper application of preventive

detention and shall be able to take legal proceedings for the effective protection of their fundamental rights.

2. In imposing penalties laid down by general law on members of these populations account shall be taken of the degree of cultural development of the populations concerned.

3. Preference shall be given to methods of rehabilitation rather than confinement in prison.

PART II. LAND

Article 11

The right of ownership, collective or individual, of the members of the populations concerned over the lands which these populations traditionally occupy shall be recognised.

Article 12

1. The populations concerned shall not be removed without their free consent from their habitual territories except in accordance with national laws and regulations for reasons relating to national security, or in the interest of national economic development or of the health of the said populations.

2. When in such cases removal of these populations is necessary as an exceptional measure, they shall be provided with lands of quality at least equal to that of the lands previously occupied by them, suitable to provide for their present needs and future development. In cases where chances of alternative employment exist and where the populations concerned prefer to have compensation in money or in kind, they shall be so compensated under appropriate guarantees.

3. Persons thus removed shall be fully compensated for any resulting loss or injury.

Article 13

1. Procedures for the transmission of rights of ownership and use of land which are established by the customs of the populations concerned shall be respected, within the framework of national laws and regulations, in so far as they satisfy the needs of these populations and do not hinder their economic and social development.

2. Arrangements shall be made to prevent persons who are not members of the populations concerned from taking advantage of these

customs or of lack of understanding of the laws on the part of the
members of these populations to secure the ownership or use of the
lands belonging to such members.

Article 14

National agrarian programmes shall secure to the populations
concerned treatment equivalent to that accorded to other sections of
the national community with regard to—

(a) the provision of more land for these populations when they have
not the area necessary for providing the essentials of a normal
existence, or for any possible increase in their numbers;

(b) the provision of the means required to promote the development
of the lands which these populations already possess.

PART III. RECRUITMENT AND CONDITIONS OF EMPLOYMENT

Article 15

1. Each Member shall, within the framework of national laws and
regulations, adopt special measures to ensure the effective protection
with regard to recruitment and conditions of employment of workers
belonging to the populations concerned so long as they are not in a
position to enjoy the protection granted by law to workers in general.

2. Each Member shall do everything possible to prevent all
discrimination between workers belonging to the populations
concerned and other workers, in particular as regards—

(a) admission to employment, including skilled employment;
(b) equal remuneration for work of equal value;
(c) medical and social assistance, the prevention of employment
injuries, workmen's compensation, industrial hygiene and housing;
(d) the right of association and freedom for all lawful trade union
activities, and the right to conclude collective agreements with
employers or employers' organisations.

PART IV. VOCATIONAL TRAINING, HANDICRAFTS AND RURAL INDUSTRIES

Article 16

Persons belonging to the populations concerned shall enjoy the
same opportunities as other citizens in respect of vocational training
facilities.

Article 17

1. Whenever programmes of vocational training of general application do not meet the special needs of persons belonging to the populations concerned governments shall provide special training facilities for such persons.

2. These special training facilities shall be based on a careful study of the economic environment, stage of cultural development and practical needs of the various occupational groups among the said populations; they shall, in particular, enable the persons concerned to receive the training necessary for occupations for which these populations have traditionally shown aptitude.

3. These special training facilities shall be provided only so long as the stage of cultural development of the populations concerned requires them; with the advance of the process of integration they shall be replaced by the facilities provided for other citizens.

Article 18

1. Handicrafts and rural industries shall be encouraged as factors in the economic development of the populations concerned in a manner which will enable these populations to raise their standard of living and adjust themselves to modern methods of production and marketing.

2. Handicrafts and rural industries shall be developed in a manner which preserves the cultural heritage of these populations and improves their artistic values and particular modes of cultural expression.

PART V. SOCIAL SECURITY AND HEALTH

Article 19

Existing social security schemes shall be extended progressively, where practicable, to cover—

(a) wage earners belonging to the populations concerned;
(b) other persons belonging to these populations.

Article 20

1. Governments shall assume the responsibility for providing adequate health services for the populations concerned.

2. The organisation of such services shall be based on systematic studies of the social, economic and cultural conditions of the populations concerned.

3. The development of such services shall be co-ordinated with general measures of social, economic and cultural development.

PART VI. EDUCATION AND MEANS OF COMMUNICATION

Article 21

Measures shall be taken to ensure that members of the populations concerned have the opportunity to acquire education at all levels on an equal footing with the rest of the national community.

Article 22

1. Education programmes for the populations concerned shall be adapted, as regards methods and techniques, to the stage these populations have reached in the process of social, economic and cultural integration in the national community.

2. The formulation of such programmes shall normally be preceded by ethnological surveys.

Article 23

1. Children belonging to the populations concerned shall be taught to read and write in their mother tongue or, where this is not practicable, in the language most commonly used by the group to which they belong.

2. Provision shall be made for a progressive transition from the mother tongue or the vernacular language to the national language or to one of the official languages of the country.

3. Appropriate measures shall, as far as possible, be taken to preserve the mother tongue or the vernacular language.

Article 24

The imparting of general knowledge and skills that will help children to become integrated into the national community shall be an aim of primary education for the populations concerned.

Article 25

Educational measures shall be taken among other sections of the national community and particularly among those that are in most direct contact with the populations concerned with the object of eliminating prejudices that they may harbour in respect of these populations.

Article 26

1. Governments shall adopt measures, appropriate to the social and cultural characteristics of the populations concerned, to make known to them their rights and duties, especially in regard to labour and social welfare.

2. If necessary this shall be done by means of written translations and through the use of media of mass communication in the languages of these populations.

PART VII. ADMINISTRATION

Article 27

1. The governmental authority responsible for the matters covered in this Convention shall create or develop agencies to administer the programmes involved.

2. These programmes shall include—

(a) planning, co-ordination and execution of appropriate measures for the social, economic and cultural development of the populations concerned;

(b) proposing of legislative and other measures to the competent authorities;

(c) supervision of the application of these measures.

PART VIII. GENERAL PROVISIONS

Article 28

The nature and the scope of the measures to be taken to give effect to this Convention shall be determined in a flexible manner, having regard to the conditions characteristic of each country.

Article 29

The application of the provisions of this Convention shall not affect benefits conferred on the populations concerned in pursuance of other Conventions and Recommendations.

Article 30

The formal ratifications of this Convention shall be communicated to the Director-General of the International Labour Office for registration.

Article 31

1. This Convention shall be binding only upon those Members of the International Labour Organisation whose ratifications have been registered with the Director-General.

2. It shall come into force twelve months after the date on which the ratifications of two Members have been registered with the Director-General.

3. Thereafter, this Convention shall come into force for any Member twelve months after the date on which its ratification has been registered.

Article 32

1. A Member which has ratified this Convention may denounce it after the expiration of ten years from the date on which the Convention first comes into force, by an act communicated to the Director-General of the International Labour Office for registration. Such denunciation shall not take effect until one year after the date on which it is registered.

2. Each Member which has ratified this Convention and which does not, within the year following the expiration of the period of ten years mentioned in the preceding paragraph, exercise the right of denunciation provided for in this Article, will be bound for another period of ten years and, thereafter, may denounce this Convention at the expiration of each period of ten years under the terms provided for in this Article.

Article 33

1. The Director-General of the International Labour Office shall

notify all Members of the International Labour Organisation of the registration of all ratifications and denunciations communicated to him by the Members of the Organisation.

2. When notifying the Members of the Organisation of the registration of the second ratification communicated to him, the Director-General shall draw the attention of the Members of the Organisation to the date upon which the Convention will come into force.

Article 34

The Director-General of the International Labour Office shall communicate to the Secretary-General of the United Nations for registration in accordance with Article 102 of the Charter of the United Nations full particulars of all ratifications and acts of denunciation registered by him in accordance with the provisions of the preceding Articles.

Article 35

At such times as it may consider necessary the Governing Body of the International Labour Office shall present to the General Conference a report on the working of this Convention and shall examine the desirability of placing on the agenda of the Conference the question of its revision in whole or in part.

Article 36

1. Should the Conference adopt a new Convention revising this Convention in whole or in part, then, unless the new Convention otherwise provides—

(a) the ratification by a Member of the new revising Convention shall *ipso jure* involve the immediate denunciation of this Convention, notwithstanding the provisions of Article 32 above, if and when the new revising Convention shall have come into force;

(b) as from the date when the new revising Convention comes into force this Convention shall cease to be open to ratification by the Members.

2. This Convention shall in any case remain in force in its actual form and content for those Members which have ratified it but have not ratified the revising Convention.

Article 37

The English and French versions of the text of this Convention are equally authoritative.

* * *

I.L.O. Recommendation 104

RECOMMENDATION CONCERNING THE PROTECTION AND INTEGRATION OF INDIGENOUS AND OTHER TRIBAL AND SEMI-TRIBAL POPULATIONS IN INDEPENDENT COUNTRIES

The General Conference of the International Labour Organisation,

Having been convened at Geneva by the Governing Body of the International Labour Office, and having met in its Fortieth Session on 5 June 1957, and

Having decided upon the adoption of certain proposals with regard to the protection and integration of indigenous and other tribal and semi-tribal populations in independent countries, which is the sixth item on the agenda of the session, and

Having determined that these proposals shall take the form of a Recommendation, supplementing the Indigenous and Tribal Populations Convention, 1957, and

Noting that the following standards have been framed with the co-operation of the United Nations, the Food and Agriculture Organisation of the United Nations, the United Nations Educational, Scientific and Cultural Organisation and the World Health Organisation, at appropriate levels and in their respective fields, and that it is proposed to seek their continuing co-operation in promoting and securing the application of these standards,

adopts this twenty-sixth day of June of the year one thousand nine hundred and fifty-seven the following Recommendation, which may be cited as the Indigenous and Tribal Populations Recommendation, 1957:

The Conference recommends that each Member should apply the

following provisions:

I. PRELIMINARY PROVISIONS

1. (1) This Recommendation applies to—

(a) members of tribal or semi-tribal populations in independent countries whose social and economic conditions are at a less advanced stage than the stage reached by the other sections of the national community, and whose status is regulated wholly or partially by their own customs or traditions or by special laws or regulations;

(b) members of tribal or semi-tribal populations in independent countries which are regarded as indigenous on account of their descent from the populations which inhabited the country, or a geographical region to which the country belongs, at the time of conquest or colonisation and which, irrespective of their legal status, live more in conformity with the social, economic and cultural institutions of that time than with the institutions of the nation to which they belong.

2. For the purposes of this Recommendation, the term 'semi-tribal' includes groups and persons who, although they are in the process of losing their tribal characteristics, are not yet integrated into the national community.

3. The indigenous and other tribal or semi-tribal populations mentioned in subparagraphs (1) and (2) of this Paragraph are referred to hereinafter as 'the populations concerned'.

II. LAND

2. Legislative or administrative measures should be adopted for the regulation of the conditions, *de facto* or *de jure*, in which the populations concerned use the land.

3. (1) The populations concerned should be assured of a land reserve adequate for the needs of shifting cultivation so long as no better system of cultivation can be introduced.

(2) Pending the attainment of the objectives of a settlement policy for semi-nomadic groups, zones should be established within which the livestock of such groups can graze without hindrance.

4. Members of the populations concerned should receive the same treatment as other members of the national population in relation to

the ownership of underground wealth or to preference rights in the development of such wealth.

5. (1) Save in exceptional circumstances defined by law the direct or indirect lease of lands owned by members of the populations concerned to persons or bodies not belonging to these populations should be restricted.

(2) In cases in which such lease is allowed, arrangements should be made to ensure that the owners will be paid equitable rents. Rents paid in respect of collectively owned land should be used, under appropriate regulations, for the benefit of the groups which owns it.

6. The mortgaging of land owned by members of the populations concerned to a person or body not belonging to these populations should be restricted.

7. Appropriate measures should be taken for the elimination of indebtedness among farmers belonging to the populations concerned. Co-operative systems of credit should be organised, and low-interest loans, technical aid and, where appropriate, subsidies, should be extended to these farmers to enable them to develop their lands.

8. Where appropriate, modern methods of co-operative production, supply and marketing should be adapted to the traditional forms of communal ownership and use of land and production implements among the populations concerned and to their traditional systems of community service and mutual aid.

III. RECRUITMENT AND CONDITIONS OF EMPLOYMENT

9. So long as the populations concerned are not in a position to enjoy the protection granted by law to workers in general, recruitment of workers belonging to these populations should be regulated by providing, in particular, for—

(a) licensing of private recruiting agents and supervision of their activities;

(b) safeguards against the disruptive influence of the recruitment of workers on their family and community life, including measures—

   (i) prohibiting recruitment during specified periods and in specified areas;
   (ii) enabling workers to maintain contact with, and participate in important tribal activities of, their communities of origin; and
   (iii) ensuring protection of the dependants of recruited workers;

(c) fixing the minimum age for recruitment and establishing special conditions for the recruitment of non-adult workers;

(d) establishing health criteria to be fulfilled by workers at the time of recruitment;

(e) establishing standards for the transport of recruited workers;

(f) ensuring that the worker—
  (i) understands the conditions of his employment, as a result of explanation in his mother tongue;
  (ii) freely and knowingly accepts the conditions of his employment.

10. So long as the populations concerned are not in a position to enjoy the protection granted by law to workers in general, the wages and the personal liberty of workers belonging to these populations should be protected, in particular, by providing that—

(a) wages shall normally be paid only in legal tender;

(b) the payment of any part of wages in the form of alcohol or other spirituous beverages or noxious drugs shall be prohibited;

(c) the payment of wages in taverns or stores, except in the case of workers employed therein, shall be prohibited;

(d) the maximum amounts and manner of repayment of advances on wages and the extent to which and conditions under which deductions from wages may be permitted shall be regulated;

(e) work stores or similar services operated in connection with the undertaking shall be supervised;

(f) the withholding or confiscation of effects and tools which workers commonly use, on the ground of debt or unfulfilled labour contract, without prior approval of the competent judicial or administrative authority shall be prohibited;

(g) interference with the personal liberty of workers on the ground of debt shall be prohibited.

11. The right to repatriation to the community of origin, at the expense of the recruiter or the employer, should be ensured in all cases where the worker—

(a) becomes incapacitated by sickness or accident during the journey to the place of employment or in the course of employment;

(b) is found on medical examination to be unfit for employment;

(c) is not engaged, after having been sent forward for engagement, for

a reason for which he is not responsible;

(d) is found by the competent authority to have been recruited by misrepresentation or mistake.

12. (1) Measures should be taken to facilitate the adaptation of workers belonging to the populations concerned to the concepts and methods of industrial relations in a modern society.

(2) Where necessary, standard contracts of employment should be drawn up in consultation with representatives of the workers and employers concerned. Such contracts should set out the respective rights and obligations of workers and employers, together with the conditions under which the contracts may be terminated. Adequate measures should be taken to ensure observance of these contracts.

13. (1) Measures should be adopted, in conformity with the law, to promote the stabilisation of workers and their families in or near employment centres, where such stabilisation is in the interests of the workers and of the economy of the countries concerned.

(2) In applying such measures, special attention should be paid to the problems involved in the adjustment of workers belonging to the populations concerned and their families to the forms of life and work of their new social and economic environment.

14. The migration of workers belonging to the populations concerned should, when considered to be contrary to the interests of these workers and of their communities, be discouraged by measures designed to raise the standards of living in the areas which they traditionally occupy.

15. (1) Governments should establish public employment services, stationary or mobile, in areas in which workers belonging to the populations concerned are recruited in large numbers.

(2) Such services should, in addition to assisting workers to find employment and assisting employers to find workers—

(a) determine the extent to which manpower shortages existing in other regions of the country could be met by manpower available in areas inhabited by the populations concerned without social or economic disturbance in these areas;

(b) advise workers and their employers on provisions concerning them contained in laws, regulations and contracts, relating to wages, housing, benefits for employment injuries, transportation

and other conditions of employment;

(c) co-operate with the authorities responsible for the enforcement of laws or regulations ensuring the protection of the populations concerned and, where necessary, be entrusted with responsibility for the control of procedures connected with the recruitment and conditions of employment of workers belonging to these populations.

IV. VOCATIONAL TRAINING

16. Programmes for the vocational training of the populations concerned should include provision for the training of members of these populations as instructors. Instructors should be conversant with such techniques, including where possible an understanding of anthropological and psychological factors, as would enable them to adapt their teaching to the particular conditions and needs of these populations.

17. The vocational training of members of the populations concerned should, as far as practicable, be carried out near the place where they live or in the place where they work.

18. During the early stages of integration this training should be given, as far as possible, in the vernacular language of the group concerned.

19. Programmes for the vocational training of the populations concerned should be co-ordinated with measures of assistance enabling independent workers to acquire the necessary materials and equipment and assisting wage earners in finding employment appropriate to their qualifications.

20. Programmes and methods of vocational training for the populations concerned should be co-ordinated with programmes and methods of fundamental education.

21. During the period of vocational training of members of the populations concerned, they should be given all possible assistance to enable them to take advantage of the facilities provided, including, where feasible, scholarships.

V. HANDICRAFTS AND RURAL INDUSTRIES

22. Programmes for the promotion of handicrafts, and rural

159

industries among the populations concerned should, in particular, aim at—

(a) improving techniques and methods of work as well as working conditions;

(b) developing all aspects of production and marketing, including credit facilities, protection against monopoly controls and against exploitation by middlemen, provision of raw materials at equitable prices, establishment of standards of craftsmanship, and protection of designs and of special aesthetic features of products; and

(c) encouraging the formation of co-operatives.

VI. SOCIAL SECURITY AND MEASURES OF ASSISTANCE

23. The extension of social security schemes to workers belonging to the populations concerned should be preceded or accompanied, as conditions may require, by measures to improve their general social and economic conditions.

24. In the case of independent primary producers provision should be made for—

(a) instruction in modern methods of farming;

(b) supply of equipment, for example implements, stocks, seeds; and

(c) protection against the loss of livelihood resulting from natural hazards to crops or stock.

VII. HEALTH

25. The populations concerned should be encouraged to organise in their communities local health boards or committees to look after the health of their members. The formation of these bodies should be accompanied by a suitable educational effort to ensure that full advantage is taken of them.

26. (1) Special facilities should be provided for the training of members of the populations concerned as auxiliary health workers and professional medical and sanitary personnel, where these members are not in a position to acquire such training through the ordinary facilities of the country.

(2) Care should be taken to ensure that the provision of special

facilities does not have the effect of depriving members of the populations concerned of the opportunity to obtain their training through the ordinary facilities.

27. The professional health personnel working among the populations concerned should have training in anthropological and psychological techniques which will enable them to adapt their work to the cultural characteristics of these populations.

VIII. EDUCATION

28. Scientific research should be organised and financed with a view to determining the most appropriate methods for the teaching of reading and writing to the children belonging to the populations concerned and for the utilisation of the mother tongue or the vernacular language as a vehicle of instruction.

29. Teachers working among the populations concerned should have training in anthropological and psychological techniques which will enable them to adapt their work to the cultural characteristics of these populations. These teachers should, as far as possible, be recruited from among such populations.

30. Pre-vocational instruction, with emphasis on the teaching of subjects relating to agriculture, handicrafts, rural industries and home economics, should be introduced in the programmes of primary education intended for the populations concerned.

31. Elementary health instruction should be included in the programmes of primary education intended for the populations concerned.

32. The primary education of the populations concerned should be supplemented, as far as possible, by campaigns of fundamental education. These campaigns should be designed to help children and adults to understand the problems of their environment and their rights and duties as citizens and individuals, thereby enabling them to participate more effectively in the economic and social progress of their community.

IX. LANGUAGES AND OTHER MEANS OF COMMUNICATION

33. Where appropriate the integration of the populations concerned should be facilitated by—

Indigenous Peoples

- *(a)* enriching the technical and juridical vocabulary of their vernacular languages and dialects;

- *(b)* establishing alphabets for the writing of these languages and dialects;

- *(c)* publishing in these languages and dialects readers adapted to the educational and cultural level of the populations concerned; and

- *(d)* publishing bilingual dictionaries.

34. Methods of audio-visual communication should be employed as means of information among the populations concerned.

X. Tribal Groups in Frontier Zones

35. (1) Where appropriate and practicable, intergovernmental action should be taken, by means of agreements between the governments concerned, to protect semi-nomadic tribal groups whose traditional territories lie across international boundaries.

(2) Such action should aim in particular at—

- *(a)* ensuring that members of these groups who work in another country receive fair wages in accordance with the standards in operation in the region of employment;

- *(b)* assisting these workers to improve their conditions of life without discrimination on account of their nationality or of their semi-nomadic character.

XI. Administration

36. Administrative arrangements should be made, either through government agencies specially created for the purpose or through appropriate co-ordination of the activities of other government agencies, for—

- *(a)* ensuring enforcement of legislative and administrative provisions for the protection and integration of the populations concerned;

- *(b)* ensuring effective possession of land and use of other natural resources by members of these populations;

- *(c)* administering the property and income of these populations when necessary in their interests;

- *(d)* providing free legal aid for the members of the populations concerned that may need legal aid but cannot afford it;

(e) establishing and maintaining educational and health services for the populations concerned;

(f) promoting research designed to facilitate understanding of the way of life of such populations and of the process of their integration into the national community;

(g) preventing the exploitation of workers belonging to the populations concerned on account of their unfamiliarity with the industrial environment to which they are introduced;

(h) where appropriate, supervising and co-ordinating, within the framework of the programmes of protection and integration, the activities, whether philanthropic or profit-making, carried out by individuals and corporate bodies, public or private, in regions inhabited by the populations concerned.

37. (1) National agencies specifically responsible for the protection and integration of the populations concerned should be provided with regional centres, situated in areas where these populations are numerous.

(2) These agencies should be staffed by officials selected and trained for the special tasks they have to perform. As far as possible, these officials should be recruited from among the members of the populations concerned.

* * *

CONCLUSIONS OF THE MEETING OF EXPERTS, 1987

EXTRACTS FROM THE REPORT OF THE MEETING OF EXPERTS ON THE REVISION OF THE INDIGENOUS AND TRIBAL POPULATIONS CONVENTION, 1957 (No. 107)

(Geneva, 1–10 September 1986)

CONCLUSIONS

1. The Convention's integrationist approach is inadequate and no longer reflects current thinking.

2. Indigenous and tribal peoples should enjoy as much control as possible over their own economic, social and cultural development.

3. The right of these peoples to interact with the national society on an equal footing through their own institutions should be recognised.

163

4. The Meeting concluded that the traditional land rights of these peoples should be recognised and effectively protected, and noted that the indigenous and tribal respresentatives present unanimously considered that these lands should be inalienable.

5. The Meeting agreed that, in order to make these rights effective, ratifying States should take measures to determine the lands to which these peoples have rights, by demarcation or delimitation where this has not already been done.

6. The authority of States to appropriate indigenous or tribal lands, or to remove these peoples from their lands, should be limited to exceptional circumstances, and should take place only with their informed consent. If this consent cannot be obtained, such authority should be exercised only after appropriate procedures designed to meet the exceptional circumstances for such taking and which guarantee to these peoples the opportunity to be effectively represented.

7. In cases where the appropriation or removals referred to in the previous paragraph proves necessary after these procedures, these groups should receive compensation including lands of at least equal extent, quality and legal status which allow the continuation of their traditional lifestyles and which are suitable to provide for their present needs and future development.

8. In all activities proposed to be taken by the ILO or by ratifying States affecting indigenous and tribal peoples these peoples should be integrally involved at every level of the process.

9. The Meeting noted that the indigenous and tribal representatives present unanimously stressed the importance of self-determination in economic, social and cultural affairs as a right and as a basic principle for the development of new standards within the ILO.

RECOMMENDATIONS

The Meeting of Experts recommends to the Governing Body:

(a) that it place the revision of this instrument on the agenda of the International Labour Conference in 1988 or as early as possible thereafter;

(b) that full account should be taken of the views expressed at this Meeting in revising the Convention;

(c) that the scope of the revision should be limited to social, economic and cultural considerations;

(d) that it take all possible measures to ensure the participation of indigenous and tribal representatives in the process leading to the revision of this Convention and in other ILO activities in this field;

(e) that the ILO should adopt a programme of activities for the protection of the rights and interests of indigenous and tribal peoples, taking account of the above-mentioned conclusions.

Annex II:

Extracts from relevant UN Working Group on Indigenous Populations documents

1. E/CN.4/Sub.2/AC.4/1985/WP.5

Introduction

1. The creation of the Working Group on Indigenous Populations was proposed by the Sub-Commission on Prevention of Discrimination and Protection of Minorities in its resolution 2 (XXXIV) of 8 September 1981, endorsed by the Commission on Human Rights in its resolution 1982/19 of 10 March 1982 and authorised by the Economic and Social Council in its resolution 1982/34 of 7 May 1982. In that resolution the Council authorised the Sub-Commission to establish annually a Working Group on Indigenous Populations to meet for up to five working days before the annual sessions of the Sub-Commission in order to:

(a) Review developments pertaining to the promotion and protection of human rights and fundamental freedoms of indigenous populations, including information requested by the Secretary-General annually from Governments, specialised agencies, regional intergovernmental organisations and non-governmental organisations in consultative status, particularly those of indigenous peoples, to analyse such materials, and to submit its conclusions to the Sub-Commission, bearing in mind the report of the Special Rapporteur of the Sub-Commission;

(b) Give special attention to the evolution of standards concerning the rights of indigenous populations, taking account of both the similarities and the differences in the situations and aspirations of indigenous populations throughout the world.

2.   The outgoing Chairman of the Sub-Commission at its thirty-seventh session, in consultation with the geographical groups, appointed Mr. Miguel Alfonso Martínez, Mrs. Erica-Irene Daes, Mrs. Gu Yijie, Mr. Kwesi B. S. Simpson and Mr. Ivan Toševski to serve on the Working Group on Indigenous Populations, during its fourth session in 1985.

3.   The Working Group held eleven public meetings from 29 July to 2 August and on 5 August 1985.

Election of Officers

4.   At its first meeting, on 29 July 1985, the Working Group by acclamation elected Mrs. Erica-Irene A. Daes as Chairman–Rapporteur.

Participation in the session

5.   The session was attended by Mr. Miguel Alfonso Martínez, Mrs. Erica-Irene Daes, Mrs. Gu Yijie, Mr. Kwesi B. S. Simpson and Mr. Ivan Toševski.

6.   The following States Members of the United Nations were represented by observers: Argentina, Australia, Bangladesh, Brazil, Canada, China, France, Honduras, India, Indonesia, Mexico, Nicaragua, New Zealand, Norway, Peru, Sri Lanka, Sweden, Turkey, United States of America and Vietnam. The Holy See was also represented by an observer.

7.   The following United Nations specialised agency was represented during the session: International Labour Organisation.

8.   The following non-governmental organisations in consultative status with the Economic and Social Council were represented:

   (a) *Indigenous Peoples' NGOs:* Four Directions Council, Indigenous World Association, International Indian Treaty Council, Indian Law Resource Centre, Indian Council of South America (CISA), Inuit Circumpolar Conference, National Aboriginal and Islander Legal Service Secretariat, National Indian Youth Council and World Council of Indigenous Peoples.

   (b) *Other NGOs:* World Federation of United Nations Associations (WFUNA), Amnesty International, Anti-Slavery Society for the Protection of Human Rights, Baha'i International Community, Commission of the Churches on International Affairs, International Association of Penal Law, International Federation of Human Rights, International Movement for Fraternal Union Among Races and Peoples, International Union for Conservation of Nature and Natural Resources, Pax Christi International, Defence for Children International, International Federation for the Protection of the Rights of Ethnic, Religious, Linguistic and other Minorities, International Human Rights Internship Program, International League for the

167

Rights and Liberation of Peoples, International Law Association, Procedural Aspects of International Law Institute, and Survival International.

9. The following indigenous people's organisations, as well as other organisations, were represented at the session and furnished information to the Working Group with its consent.

(a) *Indigenous peoples' organisations:* Aboriginal Development Services of Bangladesh, Ad Mapu Chile, Alaska Native Brotherhood, Alaska Native Foundation, Alianza de Profesionales Indigenas Bilingues, Asociación Interetnica de Desarrollo de la Selva Peruana (AIDESEP), Chakma People from Chittagong Hill Tracts, Coalition of First Nations, Central Indigena del Oriente Boliviano, Comité Exterior Mapuche, Comunidad Indígena Maskery, Confederación Campesina Indígena del Perú, Confederación de Nacionalidades Indígenas de la Amazonía Equatoriana, Coordinadora Regional de Pueblo Indio (CORPI), Cordillera Peoples Alliance, Council of Conne River Micmacs (Newfoundland, Canada), Dene Nation of Canada, Ermineskin Indian Nation, Grand Council of the Crees (Quebec, Grand Council Treaty No. 3 (Canada), Haudenosaunee, Hobbema Four Nations, Indigenous Survival International, Inuit Tapirisat of Canada (ITC, Knikathu Alaska Native Village Corporation), Louis Bull Indian Nation, Metis National Council/Canada, Miskitu People of Nicaragua, Misurasata, Montana Indian Nation, Movimiento de la Juventud Kuna, Movimiento Independiente Ecuador Ayllu, National Aboriginal and Islander Health Organisation, National Federation of Land Councils, Native Council of Canada, Native Women's Association of Canada, New South Wales Aboriginal Land Council, Nordic Sami Council, Sovereignty for Hawaii Committee, Tasmanian Aboriginal Centre, Toledo Maya Cultural Council, Union de Comuneros 'EMILIANO ZAPATA' de Michoacan, Unión de Naciones Indígenas (UNI) de Brazil, Western Shoshone Nation and Zapotec Nations.

(b) *Other organisations and institutions:* Academia de la Lengua y la Cultura Guainía, American Friends Service Committee, Asociacíon Nacional de Apoyo al Indio, Asociacíon Diffusion INTI Et Bulletin Amérique Indienne, Centre for Tribal Conscientization, Center for World Indigenous Studies, Commission Pro Indio de Sao Paulo, Comisión Permanente por la Vivienda y la Familia Indígena, Comité Belge–Amérique Indienne, Education Secretariat Affiliated A.F.M., Free Papua Movement, Gesellschaft Für Bedrohte Völker, Grupo de Trabajo – Ecuador, Incomindios Schweiz, Indigenous Peoples' Research Documentation and Information Center (DOCIP), International Association Against Torture, Informationzentrale Für Nordamerikanische Indianer, International Centre for Constitutional

Studies, International Scholars for Indigenous Americans (ISIA), International Work Group for Indigenous Affairs (IWGIA) (Denmark), Svensk Indiaska Forbundet (Sweden), Workgroup on Indigenous Peoples (Netherlands).

In addition, several participants in the Special Course on Indigenous Peoples in International Law at the 'Chateau de Bossey', near Geneva, as well as scholars and individual experts attended the meetings. All in all, approximately 250 persons took part in the session.

* * *

2. E/CN.4/Sub.2/AC.4/1985/WP.5

After considering the comments and information submitted by Governments and indigenous organisations since its establishment, the Working Group discussed, in the course of several private meetings held during the present session, how to continue its immediate future work on standard-setting in accordance with its mandate as laid down in resolution 1982/34 of the Economic and Social Council, and on the basis of operative paragraph 8 of Sub-Commission resolution 1984/35-B. It was agreed to proceed as follows.[1]

The Working Group should aim at producing, in due course, and as a first formal step, a draft declaration on indigenous rights, which may be proclaimed by the General Assembly.

As a point of departure in that process, the Working Group should take due account of the international instruments already existing on this subject within the United Nations system, particularly those which make up the International Bill of Human Rights, and proceed on the basis of opinions advanced by both Governments and indigenous organisations.

Governments and indigenous organisations should be encouraged to submit comments and suggestions on the drafts prepared by the Working Group. Their special attention should be drawn, in anticipation of the Working Group's fifth session in 1986, to the following rights already proposed and discussed, in a preliminary manner, at the Working Group's previous sessions:

---

1. One member of the Working Group was not present when this decision was taken.

Indigenous Peoples

Draft Principles
(preliminary wording)

1. The right to the full and effective enjoyment of the fundamental rights and freedoms universally recognised in existing international instruments, particularly in the Charter of the United Nations and the International Bill of Human Rights.

2. The right to be free and equal to all other human beings in dignity and rights, and to be free from discrimination of any kind.

3. The collective right to exist and to be protected against genocide, as well as the individual right to life, physical integrity, liberty, and security of person.

4. The right to manifest, teach, practise and observe their own religious traditions and ceremonies, and to maintain, protect, and have access to sites for these purposes.

5. The right to all forms of education, including the right to have access to education in their own languages, and to establish their own educational institutions.

6. The right to preserve their cultural identity and traditions, and to pursue their own cultural development.

7. The right to promote intercultural information and education, recognising the dignity and diversity of their cultures.

*   *   *

3. E/CN.4/Sub.2/AC.4/1985/WP.5

Declaration of principles adopted at the Fourth General Assembly of the World Council of Indigenous Peoples in Panama, September 1984[1]

Principle 1. All indigenous peoples have the right of self-determination. By virtue of this right they may freely determine their political status and freely pursue their economic, social, religious and cultural development.

Principle 2. All States within which an indigenous peoples lives shall recognise the population, territory and institutions of the indigenous people.

Principle 3. The cultures of the indigenous peoples are part of the cultural heritage of mankind.

---

1 Appeared also in document E/CN.4/Sub.2/AC.4/1985/WP.4 and Corr.1.

170

Principle 4.　The traditions and customs of indigenous people must be respected by the States, and recognised as a fundamental source of law.

Principle 5.　All indigenous peoples have the right to determine the person or group of persons who are included within its population.

Principle 6.　Each indigenous people has the right to determine the form, structure and authority of its institutions.

Principle 7.　The institutions of indigenous peoples and their decisions, like those of States, must be in conformity with internationally accepted human rights both collective and individual.

Principle 8.　Indigenous peoples and their members are entitled to participate in the political life of the State.

Principle 9.　Indigenous people shall have exclusive rights to their traditional lands and its resources, where the lands and resources of the indigenous peoples have been taken away without their free and informed consent such lands and resources shall be returned.

Principle 10.　The land rights of an indigenous people include surface and subsurface rights, full rights to interior and coastal waters and rights to adequate and exclusive coastal economic zones within the limits of international law.

Principle 11.　All indigenous peoples may, for their own needs, freely use their natural wealth and resources in accordance with Principles 9 and 10.

Principle 12.　No action or course of conduct may be undertaken which, directly or indirectly, may result in the destruction of land, air, water, sea ice, wildlife, habitat or natural resources without the free and informed consent of the indigenous peoples affected.

Principle 13.　The original rights to their material culture, including archaeological sites, artifacts, designs, technology and works of art, lie with the indigenous people.

Principle 14.　The indigenous peoples have the right to receive education in their own language or to establish their own educational institutions. The languages of the indigenous peoples are to be respected by the States in all dealings between the indigenous people and the State on the basis of equality and non-discrimination.

Principle 15.　Indigenous peoples have the right, in accordance with their traditions, to move and conduct traditional activities and maintain friendship relations across international boundaries.

Principle 16.　The indigenous peoples and their authorities have the right to be previously consulted and to authorise the realisation of all technological and scientific investigations to be conducted within their territories and to have full access to the results of the investigation.

Indigenous Peoples

Principle 17.   Treaties between indigenous nations or peoples and
representatives of States freely entered into, shall be given full effect
under national and international law.

These principles constitute the minimum standards which States shall
respect and implement.

* * *

4. E/CN.4/Sub.2/AC.4/1985/WP.5

Draft declaration of principles proposed by the Indian Law Resource
Center, Four Directions Council, National Aboriginal and Islander
Legal Service, National Indian Youth Council, Inuit Circumpolar
Conference, and the International Indian Treaty Council[1]

Declaration of principles

1.   Indigenous nations and peoples have, in common with all
humanity, the right to life, and to freedom from oppression,
discrimination, and aggression.
2.   All indigenous nations and peoples have the right to self-
determination, by virtue of which they have the right to whatever
degree of autonomy or self-government they choose. This includes the
right to freely determine their political status, freely pursue their own
economic, social, religious and cultural development, and determine
their own membership and/or citizenship, without external interference.
3.   No State shall assert any jurisdiction over an indigenous nation or
people, or its territory, except in accordance with the freely expressed
wishes of the nation or people concerned.
4.   Indigenous nations and peoples are entitled to the permanent
control and enjoyment of their aboriginal ancestral–historical
territories. This includes surface and subsurface rights, inland and
coastal waters, renewable and non-renewable resources, and the
economies based on these resources.
5.   Rights to share and use land, subject to the underlying and
inalienable title of the indigenous nation or people, may be granted by
their free and informed consent, as evidenced in a valid treaty or
agreement.

---

1 Appeared also in document E/CN.4/Sub.2/AC.4/1985/WP.4/Add.4.

6.   Discovery, conquest, settlement on a theory of *terra nullius* and unilateral legislation are never legitimate bases for States to claim or retain the territories of indigenous nations or peoples.

7.   In cases where lands taken in violation of these principles have already been settled, the indigenous nation or people concerned is entitled to immediate restitution, including compensation for the loss of use, without extinction of original title. Indigenous peoples' desire to regain possession and control of sacred sites must always be respected.

8.   No State shall participate financially or militarily in the involuntary displacement of indigenous populations, or in the subsequent economic exploitation or military use of their territory.

9.   The laws and customs of indigenous nations and peoples must be recognised by States' legislative, administrative and judicial institutions and, in case of conflicts with State laws, shall take precedence.

10.   No State shall deny an indigenous nation, community, or people residing within its borders the right to participate in the life of the State in whatever manner and to whatever degree they may choose. This includes the right to participate in other forms of collective action and expression.

11.   Indigenous nations and peoples continue to own and control their material culture, including archaeological, historical and sacred sites, artifacts, designs, knowledge, and works of art. They have the right to regain items of major cultural significance and, in all cases, to the return of the human remains of their ancestors for burial in accordance with their traditions.

12.   Indigenous nations and peoples have the right to be educated and conduct business with States in their own languages, and to establish their own educational institutions.

13.   No technical, scientific or social investigations, including archaeological excavations, shall take place in relation to indigenous nations or peoples, or their lands, without their prior authorisation, and their continuing ownership and control.

14.   The religious practices of indigenous nations and peoples shall be fully respected and protected by the laws of States and by international law. Indigenous nations and peoples shall always enjoy unrestricted access to, and enjoyment of sacred sites in accordance with their own laws and customs, including the right of privacy.

15.   Indigenous nations and peoples are subjects of international law.

16.   Treaties and other agreements freely made with indigenous nations or peoples shall be recognised and applied in the same manner and according to the same international laws and principles as treaties and agreements entered into with other States.

17.   Disputes regarding the jurisdiction, territories and institutions of

an indigenous nation or people are a proper concern of international law, and must be resolved by mutual agreement or valid treaty.

18.   Indigenous nations and peoples may engage in self-defence against State actions in conflict with their right to self-determination.

19.   Indigenous nations and peoples have the right freely to travel, and to maintain economic, social, cultural and religious relations with each other across State borders.

20.   In addition to these rights, indigenous nations and peoples are entitled to the enjoyment of all the human rights and fundamental freedoms enumerated in the international Bill of Rights and other United Nations instruments. In no circumstances shall they be subjected to adverse discrimination.

Annex III:

Information Note on the Independent Commission on International Humanitarian Issues

The establishment of an Independent Commission on International Humanitarian Issues is the response of a group of eminent persons from all parts of the world to the deeply felt need to enhance public awareness of important humanitarian issues and to promote an international climate favouring progress in the humanitarian field.

The work of the Commission is intended to be a part of the continuing search of the world community for a more adequate international framework to uphold human dignity and rise to the challenge of colossal humanitarian problems arising with increasing frequency in all continents.

In 1981, the UN General Assembly adopted by consensus a resolution relating to a New International Humanitarian Order in which it recognised: 'The importance of further improving a comprehensive international framework which takes fully into account existing instruments relating to humanitarian questions as well as the need for addressing those aspects which are not yet adequately covered.' In doing so, the Assembly bore in mind that 'institutional arrangements and actions of governmental and non-governmental bodies might need to be further strengthened to respond effectively in situations requiring humanitarian action.'

The following year, the General Assembly adopted by consensus a further resolution relating to the International Humanitarian Order in which it noted 'the proposal for establishment, outside the United Nations framework, of an Independent Commission on International Humanitarian Issues composed of leading personalities in the humanitarian field or having wide experience of government or world affairs.'

175

Indigenous Peoples

The Independent Commission on International Humanitarian Issues was established in 1983 and held its first plenary meeting in New York in November that year. A few days later, the UN General Assembly adopted another resolution in which it noted the establishment of the Commission and requested the Secretary-General to remain in contact with governments as well as the Independent Commission in order to provide a comprehensive report on the subject to the Assembly.

In 1985, the Secretary-General presented to the General Assembly his report as well as comments from governments on the New International Humanitarian Order. The report included a description of the Independent Commission and its work. In a subsequent resolution adopted by consensus, the General Assembly took note of the activities of the Commission and looked forward to the outcome of its efforts and its Final Report.

Composition of the Commission

The Commission is an independent body whose members participate in their personal capacity and not as representatives of governments or international bodies to which they may belong. Its work is not intended to interfere with governmental negotiations or inter-state relations, nor to duplicate work being done by existing governmental or non-governmental bodies.

In its deliberations, the Commission benefits from the advice of governments, existing international governmental and non-governmental bodies and leading experts. The composition of the Commission is limited and based on equitable geographical distribution. It has twenty-eight members. Details regarding the members are to be found at the end of this note.

The Purpose of the Commission

The Purpose of the Commission is:

* to study specific humanitarian issues that have been inadequately dealt with to date, or call for solutions in line with new realities;

* to identify opportunities for more effective action by the international community and to make practical, action-oriented proposals that promote the well-being of people;

* to enhance public awareness of the conditions that create and perpetuate human suffering, and to strengthen efforts, at governmental and non-governmental level to bring about changes that will help make the world a more humane place.

The Work of the Commission is determined by the desire to be realistic, pragmatic and innovative. During its limited life-span of three years, the Commission is focusing on three broad areas of concern.

Humanitarian Norms in the context of armed conflicts. Although considerable progress has been made in developing and codifying international humanitarian law, flagrant disregard of humanitarian norms persists. This reality spells heightened dangers for the victims of armed conflicts, an increasing number of whom are civilians. The aim of the Commission, on the one hand, is to actively encourage adhesion by governments to existing international instruments and, on the other, to propose measures that deal with new problems arising out of contemporary armed conflicts.

Disasters, natural and man-made, are not a new phenomenon. But their debilitating frequency and catastrophic consequences provoke pertinent questions as to our ability and willingness to address the root causes of such calamities. The new humanitarian crises demonstrate the necessity of new perspectives and approaches in translating the short-term relief efforts of today into long-term strategies that safeguard the welfare of future generations. The factors which create disasters – and most cannot simply be attributed to the caprices of nature – are many and complex. The Commission, therefore, has selected a number of inter-related issues that are central to disaster prevention and preparedness. Particularly concerned about the destruction of the earth's resources, the Commission has focused on the humanitarian aspects of problems such as desertification, deforestation, famine as well as such man-made disasters as nuclear and industrial accidents.

Vulnerable Groups is a term attributed to many who suffer deprivation by virtue of their status in society. However, given that the Commission's work is limited in time and scope, it has concentrated on the plight of only a few of the unprotected or vulnerable groups in specific situations of disaster or acute hardship. These include the stateless, the disappeared, refugees and displaced persons, indigenous populations, street children and the urban young. The Commission's purpose is to study the problems unique to each group, the deprivation entailed, the lack of an adequate international response, and the practical measures which could be taken to lessen their hardship.

In addition to analysing and making recommendations on specific issues, sensitising public opinion, and reminding Governments of their humanitarian obligations, the Commission will, upon completion of its deliberations, make a Final Report. It will be policy and action-oriented, with specific proposals on how a more humanitarian response can be developed by governments and the international community.

The Commission operates through a small secretariat in Geneva which co-ordinates research activities and services the work of the Commission. The reports on specific topics addressed by the Commission are formulated after in-depth study by the Commission Members. Working Groups, composed of Members with special interest or expertise in the subject, assisted by a group of recognised experts, have been established to investigate different issues. The Working Groups collaborate closely through the secretariat with the relevant academic centres as well as governmental and non-governmental international bodies. Experts as well as representatives of the international bodies concerned are also invited, as appropriate, to participate in the deliberations of the Commission or the Working Groups.

This process ensures that the Commission's activities do not duplicate the work of other organisations but rather complement the on-going search for better and more effective solutions to humanitarian problems. Draft reports are then reviewed by all the Commission Members. When finalised, they are made public as 'sectoral reports' prepared for the Commission. A list of these sectoral reports is to be found at the beginning of this book.

Periodically, the Commission organises seminars, expert consultations, brain-storming sessions and public meetings to examine issues or to make its views known. This process also promotes a greater awareness and understanding of humanitarian questions.

The work of the Commission is funded by government contributions and private sources.

Members of the Commission

Sadruddin AGA KHAN (Iran) – UN High Commissioner for Refugees, 1965–77; Special Consultant to the UN Secretary-General since 1978. Special Rapporteur of the UN Human Rights Commission, 1981. Founder–President of the Bellerive Group.

Susanna AGNELLI (Italy) – Under-Secretary of State for Foreign Affairs since 1983. Member of the Italian Senate. Member of the European Parliament, 1979–81. Journalist and author.

Talal Bin Abdul Aziz AL SAUD (Saudi Arabia) – President, the Arab Gulf Programme for UN Development Organisations (AGFUND). UNICEF's Special Envoy, 1980–84. Former Minister of Communications, of Finance and National Economy and Vice-President of the Supreme Planning Commission.

Paulo Evaristo ARNS (Brazil) – Cardinal, Archbishop of Sao Paulo. Chancellor of the Pontifical Catholic University, Sao Paulo State. Author.

Mohammed BEDJAOUI (Algeria) – Judge at the International Court of Justice since 1982. Minister of Justice, 1964–70. Ambassador to France, 1970–79; UNESCO, 1971–79; and the United Nations in New York, 1979–82. Author.

Henrik BEER (Sweden) – Secretary-General of the League of Red Cross Societies, 1960–82; Secretary-General of the Swedish Red Cross, 1947–60. Member of the International Institute for Environment and Development and the International Institute of Humanitarian Law.

Igor P. BLISHCHENKO (USSR) – Chairman of the International Law Department of Patrice Lumumba University, Moscow; Professor of Legal Sciences; Member of Soviet Delegation to the Diplomatic Conference on the Reaffirmation and Development of International Humanitarian Law. Consultant to the Soviet Academy of Sciences.

Luis ECHEVERRIA ALVAREZ (Mexico) – President of the Republic, 1970–76; Founder and Director-General of the Centre for Economic and Social Studies of the Third World, 1976. Former Ambassador to Australia, New Zealand and UNESCO.

Pierre GRABER (Switzerland) – President of the Swiss Confederation, 1975; Foreign Minister, 1975–78. President of the Diplomatic Conference on the Reaffirmation and Development of International Humanitarian Law, 1974–77.

Ivan L. HEAD (Canada) – President of the International Development Research Centre (IDRC); Special Assistant to the Prime Minister of Canada, 1968–78. Queen's Counsel.

M. HIDAYATULLAH (India) – Vice-President of India, 1979–84. Former Chief Justice of the Supreme Court. Chancellor of the Jamia Millia Islamia since 1979. Former Chancellor of the Universities of Delhi, Punjab. Author.

Aziza HUSSEIN (Egypt) – Member of the Population Council. President of the International Planned Parenthood Federation, 1977–

85. Fellow of the International Peace Academy, Helsinki, 1971 and the Aspen Institute of Humanistic Studies, 1978–79.

Manfred LACHS (Poland) – Judge at the International Court of Justice since 1967 and its President, 1973–76. Professor of Political Science and International Law. Former Chairman of the UN Legal Committee on the Peaceful Uses of Outer Space. Author.

Robert S. McNAMARA (USA) – President of the World Bank, 1968–81; Secretary of Defense, 1961–68. President, Ford Motor Company, 1960–61; Trustee of the Brookings Institute, Ford Foundation, the Urban Institute and the California Institute of Technology. Author.

Lazar MOJSOV (Yugoslavia) – President of the Presidency of the Socialist Federal Republic of Yugoslavia. Former Foreign Minister. Ambassador to the USSR, Mongolia, Austria, the United Nations, 1958–74. President of the UN General Assembly, 32nd Session and of the Special Session on Disarmament, 1978.

Mohammed MZALI (Tunisia) – Former Prime Minister and General Secretary of the Destorian Socialist Party. Former Minister of National Defence, Education, Youth and Sports and Health. Author.

Sadako OGATA (Japan) – Professor at the Institute of International Relations, Sophia University, Tokyo. Representative of Japan to the United Nations Human Rights Commission. Member of the Trilateral Commission.

David OWEN (United Kingdom) – Member of Parliament since 1966. Leader of the Social Democratic Party since 1983. Foreign Secretary, 1977–79.

Willibald P. PAHR (Austria) – Secretary-General of the World Tourism Organisation. Federal Minister of Foreign Affairs, 1976–83. Ambassador. Vice-President of the International Institute of Human Rights, Strasbourg.

Shridath S. RAMPHAL (Guyana) – Secretary-General of the Commonwealth since 1975. Former Attorney-General, Foreign Minister and Minister of Justice.

RU XIN (China) – Vice-President of the Chinese Academy of Social Sciences; Professor of Philosophy at the Xiamen University; Executive President of the Chinese National Society of the History of World Philosophies.

Salim A. SALIM (Tanzania) – Deputy Prime Minister and Minister of Defence. Former Prime Minister and Foreign Minister. Ambassador to Egypt, India, China and Permanent Representative to the United Nations. Former President of the UN General Assembly and the Security Council.

Léopold Sédar SENGHOR (Senegal) – Member of the French Academy. President of the Republic of Senegal, 1960–80. Cabinet Minister in the French Government before leading his country to independence in 1960. Poet and philosopher.

SOEDJATMOKO (Indonesia) – Rector of the United Nations University, Tokyo since 1980. Ambassador to the United States. Member of the Club of Rome and Trustee of the Aspen Institute and the Ford Foundation. Author.

Hassan bin TALAL (Jordan) – Crown Prince of the Hashemite Kingdom. Founder of the Royal Scientific Society and the Arab Thought Forum. Concerned with development planning of Jordan and the formulation of national, economic and social policies. Author.

Desmond TUTU (South Africa) – Archbishop of Cape Town. Winner of Nobel Peace Prize. Former Secretary-General of the South African Council of Churches. Professor of Theology.

Simone VEIL (France) – Member of the European Parliament and its President 1979–82; Chairperson of the Legal Affairs Committee of the European Parliament. Former Minister of Health, Social Security and Family Affairs, 1974–79.

E. Gough WHITLAM (Australia) – Former Prime Minister, 1972–75; Member of Parliament, 1952–78. Former Minister of Foreign Affairs, and Ambassador to UNESCO.

Titles on Indigenous Peoples

Julian Burger
REPORT FROM THE FRONTIER
The State of the World's Indigenous Peoples
1987

Roger Moody (editor)
THE INDIGENOUS VOICE: VISIONS AND REALITIES
(in two volumes)
Forthcoming, 1988

Roxanne Dunbar Ortiz
INDIANS OF THE AMERICAS
Self-Determination and Human Rights
1985

Sue Branford and Oriel Glock
THE LAST FRONTIER
Fighting over Land in the Amazon
1985

Peter Rigby
PERSISTENT PASTORALISTS
Nomadic Societies in Transition
1985

Gérard Chaliand (editor)
PEOPLE WITHOUT A COUNTRY
The Kurds and Kurdistan
1981

Gérard Chaliand and Yves Ternon
THE ARMENIANS
From Genocide to Resistance
1984

Permanent Peoples Tribunal
A CRIME OF SILENCE
The Armenian Genocide
1985

Carmel Budiardjo and Liem Soei Liong
THE WAR AGAINST EAST TIMOR
1984

Nils-Aslak Valkeapää
GREETINGS FROM LAPPLAND
The Sami – Europe's Forgotten People
1983

David Stoll
FISHERS OF MEN OR FOUNDERS OF EMPIRE?
The Wycliffe Bible Translators in Latin America
1982.

The above titles are available in both a cased and a limp edition, and can be ordered direct from Zed Books Ltd., 57 Caledonian Road, London N1 9BU. If you are interested in a full Catalogue of Zed titles on the Third World, please write to the same address.